SINGER AND ACTOR

SINGER AND ACTOR

Acting Technique and the
Operatic Performer

ALAN E. HICKS

AMADEUS
PRESS

AN IMPRINT OF HAL LEONARD CORPORATION

Published in 2011 by Amadeus Press
An Imprint of Hal Leonard Corporation
7777 West Bluemound Road
Milwaukee, WI 53213

Trade Book Division Editorial Offices
33 Plymouth St., Montclair, NJ 07042

Printed in the United States of America

Book design by Michael Kellner

Library of Congress Cataloging-in-Publication Data

Hicks, Alan E.
  Singer and actor : acting technique and the operatic performer / Alan E. Hicks.
    p. cm.
  Includes bibliographical references and index.
  ISBN 978-1-57467-201-5
  1. Acting in opera I. Title.
  MT956.H53 2011
  792.502'8--dc23
                                    2011041505
www.amadeuspress.com

To Mom and Dad,
without whom nothing would have been possible

Contents

Preface

The journey of this book began when I was a graduate student in vocal performance at Rice University. Until that point, I had no formal training in stagecraft and, as was the case with most of my colleagues, believed opera was a "park and bark"[1] art form. After all, we had little evidence to the contrary. Pavarotti was still singing and was too big (famous and overweight) to do much more than stand in one place and sing beautifully. During a party at the house of one of my fellow students, we sat glued to the television watching a famous soprano perform in an opera in which her character was at least forty years her junior. The soprano was so overweight that her leading man could not get his arms around her. Even if she, or Pavarotti, wanted to act as the character demanded—or for that matter, walk briskly across the stage—they would likely have been too winded to sing. This was the art form to which my colleagues and I aspired. Now, for better or worse (and there would be plenty to line up on both sides of this issue), the art form has changed and continues to change.

The moment that I knew I had been wrong about singing and acting was during a workshop class in which a female colleague and I were tasked with interpreting a particular musical theatre scene. During the course of this rather frustrating rehearsal, the director asked me, "What is your objective; what do you want?" I said, "I want her to say 'Yes' and come away with me."

"No. What is it that you really want? Think *simple*."

"I want her to come away with me."

"No. It's simpler than that."

"I want her to like me."

"No! Simpler!"

"I want her to fall in love—"

"No!"

I had always considered myself a good actor. In fact, I felt I trailed my colleagues in my vocal studies (due to a late start) but could always rely on my acting ability to get by. After all, I had been in musicals, community

---

1. "Park and bark" refers to a style of operatic performance that involves standing in one place and singing, with little regard for acting.

theatre productions, and even once in a college theatre production while I was still in high school! Passion and activity (or doing a lot of "business"[2]), it seems, were not the only items necessary for good acting.

"What do you want?" she said, becoming irritated.

In my frustration, I blurted out, "I want to have sex with her!" (The word that I actually used should not be repeated in polite company.)

"Exactly! Now do it again."

Years later, while studying Shakespeare, this event became clearer to me. On the first day of class, my teacher, an actor of some forty years with whom I was fortunate enough to study, held up her Shakespeare anthology and said, "There is nothing in this book except sex, death, and a little bit of food." I remember writing in my notebook, "Acting is instinct; based on human need."

This is, of course, a tragic oversimplification, but a necessary one when dealing with people who have never studied acting. Sadly, most opera singers would fall into this category. Over the past fifteen years, as I have worked with graduates from major conservatories and schools of music, I have found that even the most revered programs do not require—or in some cases, do not offer—acting classes to their students. When I studied voice as an undergraduate and graduate, the required acting training went no further than what I learned in a class called "Opera Workshop." Fortunately, at least for me, my graduate instructor was a musical theatre veteran of some accomplishment and had come from a world in which you were expected to be a proficient actor. Most singers are not that lucky.

Even opera directors tend to shy away from requiring real acting work. During one of my first professional contracts as an assistant director, I worked with an accomplished opera director who had been an actor before coming to opera. During one of our final staging rehearsals, he told the cast, "Unlike most directors, I don't believe that the drama is as important as the music, so I have nothing more to tell you." I was stunned by this statement, and for reasons that will become evident later in this book, many composers and librettists rolled over in their collective graves at the utterance of these words. Sadly, this attitude is not uncommon among directors. In his book *The Music Theatre of Walter Felsenstein,* Peter Paul Fuchs describes a similar directorial philosophy with respect to operatic "realism."

The irony was that with some of these "realistic" directors of the past their

---

2. "Stage business" is a phrase that often refers to activities undertaken by the character (e.g., ironing, playing cards, cleaning, and so forth). It is important to remember that *acting* and *activity* are two very different things.

realism encompassed sets, costumes and lighting, but left the performers
and their "standard" operatic gestures almost untouched. I remember one
stage director who would spend sleepless nights over the placement of
every little glow-worm in the first act of *Butterfly*, but who on the other
hand would shrug off the most amateurish excesses of anti-acting on the
part of his singers.[3]

Perhaps it is the product of having been overruled by conductors and artistic
directors too many times and wishing to avoid an artistic confrontation with
the check writers. Perhaps it is the belief that directing stage "traffic" (rather
than guiding the storytelling) is all for which the director is responsible.
Perhaps some directors truly believe that the music is more important.
Though this is a common theme among directors who have been in the
opera business for many years, it is not how opera was intended to function
by its creators (this statement will be defended in the first chapter).

The great acting teacher Sanford Meisner felt that actors had essentially
two problems: they were self-conscious and they did not listen to each
other.[4] Opera singers are particularly afflicted by these issues. It is easy to
recognize singers who feel uncomfortable on stage, as they tend to close
their bodies (by clasping their hands, folding their arms, and so forth),
strike "stock" poses (such as the unfortunately named "baritone claw"), or
pace uncontrollably.

As for listening, it is often easy to look at a singer on stage, experienced
or not, and read his or her thoughts: "He's singing, he's singing, he's singing,
blah, blah, blah. Okay, now I sing." For young singers and even some singers
who have made decent careers, some of this inability to listen is related to
the fact that they do not understand what is being said to them. They have
not translated the score, are not fluent in the language of the opera, or have
only translated their roles. "Acting is reacting," I remember being told once.
As a young singer, I thought, "How can I react to what I don't understand?
They are speaking a foreign language!" Of course, therein lies the answer,
and it wasn't until I became a director that it became clear how important it
was for singers to listen, understand, and react honestly to each other.

There are many things that actors ask themselves of the work they do
that singers have been trained not to ask. Chief among those questions is
"Why?"

---

3. Peter Paul Fuchs, ed., forward in *The Music Theatre of Walter Felsenstein* (London: Quartet,
1991).
4. Sanford Meisner, Martin Barter, and Sydney Pollack, dir., *Sanford Meisner Master Class*,
(Los Angeles: Open Road Films, 2006), DVD.

Why do I say what I say?

Why do I use these specific words?

Why does my character sit and comb her hair while singing this aria?

Etc. . . .

Most singers I have worked with will take a stage direction, such as "cross down left and look into the mirror," and do just that. Some will attempt to make that motion look natural and consider said effort "acting." Most rarely ask themselves, "Why do I (the character) move at this moment?" The answer to such a question, no matter how simple, would inevitably remove the need to "act" and allow the singer to simply "be."

Too much of what singers view as the "character" is based on the technical needs of singing. In other words, singers tend to look at the score as giving them all of the information needed to assume the characters they will portray. This is evidenced in the words uttered by many singers: "I will *sing* the role of Almaviva." One can see in that seemingly innocent statement that singers are trained to believe that the singing is all that matters. This is often reinforced by voice teachers and conductors in universities whose careers (if they had them) were twenty to thirty years prior (when "park and bark" was the norm).

Singers look at the "character" as being the notes on the page and the underlying vowel and consonant combinations—not the words the character uses, but the sounds. For example, "Je veux vivre" is often seen by young sopranos as [ʒə vø vi.vrə] (i.e., the International Phonetic Alphabet [IPA] spelling used in diction classes). As I will say many times in this book and in my career, good acting is *not* the enemy of good singing. Rather, good acting can assist singing technique and has the added benefit of providing emotional context to the music being made. Yes, the composer has provided some of that emotional context in the melody, rhythm, and harmonies chosen. If that were all that were required, there would be no need for costumes, sets, or even a theatre. Patrons could experience the same effect in their cars or at home in front of a nice pair of speakers.

Following the euphoria of being offered a role, the first thing most young singers do is buy a recording (or several) and a score and spend the next several weeks listening to, but not researching, the opera. Some won't even listen to the entire opera—only the scenes in which their characters sing. The first step to understanding the role in order to do the required acting work (which, as stated earlier, helps the singing) is to research the role, adding that information to the learning of the text and music. As the saying goes, "You can't teach an old dog new tricks." It is equally difficult to fix emotional and vocal choices made based on little or no information.

When looking at undergraduate curricula in both acting and singing, we see a disparity in where attention is placed. For example, actors are required to take acting courses and voice courses (typically classes in both vocal production and voice and speech, but often singing as well). These classes are required during most if not all of the actors' time in that training program. Singers take voice lessons their entire academic careers, but most schools require less than six hours (two semesters) of acting if it is required at all. When a singer reaches graduate school as a vocal performance or opera major, often there is less emphasis placed on acting, when there should be more. Though the National Association of Schools of Music (NASM)[5] requires acting training, most schools circumvent this requirement by placing acting under the catch-all course known as "Opera Workshop." Rarely if ever do those teaching Opera Workshop teach acting, let alone an organized approach to role preparation. The simple fact of the matter is that singers need more training rather than less. Singers, even recitalists, are actors and should be trained as such. Too often, acting is left to the innate ability of the singer. Good actors remain good, but are never great. Bad actors remain bad (and often develop a defensive posture about their lack of ability).

What is the purpose of this book? Upon reading one of my assigned papers, a professor once said, "This is great. Now—so what and who cares?" Writing is not something I often do, but when I write, "so what and who cares" fuels my process. If I cannot answer that question, I do not write. My goal for this book is simply to inform singers of those tenets of *Method acting* that will benefit them in this new climate of the "total package" performer,[6] only to burden them with history as it is necessary to understand the ideas set forth, and to provide a toolbox that the singer will fill throughout his or her career. In short, I hope to make the *singer* into a *singer-actor*. I intend only to include those ideas and exercises that I have found beneficial in my performing, directing, and most of all, teaching.

It is important to note that I am sympathetic to singers and do not blame them for what they were never offered. I was, after all, a singer before I was a director and teacher. I went about my career relying on artificial, external activities that would impress the audience but really meant nothing. During my time at the American Academy of Dramatic Arts, I began to realize how

---

5. NASM sets and maintains the national standards required for the accreditation of schools of music in the United States.

6. A "total package" performer is one who has training in the vocal arts as well as the theatrical arts. The latter consists of training in acting, stage combat, dance, and period movement. The "total package" singer would also possess exquisite language and musical skills and would be healthy and in an appropriate physical condition (see the chapter on physical appropriateness).

simple it would be for an opera singer to undertake such training. However, just the thought of Method acting strikes fear in the hearts of most singers. After all, how does one reconcile the diagram found in illustration P.1 with the mental and physical techniques needed to perform that which is found in illustration P.2? My approach is to take all of the information on the subject of Method acting and boil it down to only those tenets most important to and most feasible for singers.

Many directors who preach the virtues of acting to singers are theatre directors or former actors who have never sung an operatic role on stage. This is not the case here. I was a singer before becoming a director and understand the trepidation many singers feel with regard to acting. My goal is not to make the singer's job harder. It is, instead, to make *getting the job* easier. As a friend of mine is fond of pointing out, "Work begets work." I suggest that a more accurate axiom in today's climate would be "Good work begets work."

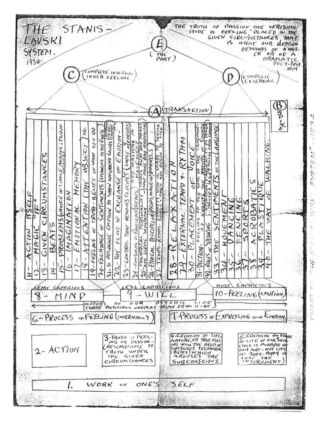

Illustration P.1: Drawing by Stella Adler titled "The Stanislavski System. 1934," held in the Stella Adler and Harold Clurman Papers Collection at the Harry Ransom Center, the University of Texas at Austin.

Illustration P.2: From Wolfgang Amadeus Mozart's *Die Zauberflöte*, "Der Hölle Rache kocht in meinem Herzen" (Queen of the Night, act 2 aria) (Bonn: N. Simrock, n.d. [ca.1793]), 84–85.

Acknowledgments

I would like to acknowledge the following people, all of whom had a hand in shaping my appreciation for and understanding of opera and theatre, or in some way contributed to my life in the arts (whether they know it or not): Franchelle ("Fran") S. Dorn, whose class on acting Shakespeare afforded me a new understanding of acting technique and its application to opera; Jay Lesenger, who gave me my first professional opportunities as a singer, and later as a director; Linda Karen Smith and William Murray, who taught me to sing; Tom Jaber, who kept me from quitting; Dr. Douglas McConnell, who taught me theory and composition; Robert Blumenfeld, whose books have had a tremendous impact on my understanding of acting, and whose championing of this book ultimately resulted in its publication; Dr. K. M. Knittel, who guided me through the writing process of the original thesis (the basis for this book); Bruce Stasyna, whose friendship and expertise as a vocal coach have been a constant source of clarity and support over the course of my career in opera; and the faculty and students of the American Academy of Dramatic Arts, a wonderful acting conservatory that inspired me at a time when I was lacking inspiration.

Introduction

In a lecture delivered at the Chautauqua Institute in 2007, Peter Gelb articulated his simple yet telling analysis of the creation of opera as it pertains to the current operatic climate: "[Opera was] meant to be . . . a pure, theatrical art form . . . a complex but perfect . . . marriage of music and theatre."[1] Gelb, who was less than a year before appointed general director of the Metropolitan Opera (one of the most influential opera houses in the world), added:

> Great artists are those who have in their vocal delivery and in their stage and in their acting the combination of all those elements that make it work . . . Looking beautiful is not enough, particularly if you can't act and certainly if you can't sing. Those artists are not going to be on the stage at the Met.[2]

The idea that operas were meant to be more than just "sonatinas for the throat" can be seen throughout history in the writings of those responsible for the art form—composers and librettists. Pietro Metastasio, the eighteenth century's most prolific librettist, believed that the only way to keep the art form alive was "through proper training in acting [and] proper concern for the synthesis of *canto* and *azione* (singing and acting)."[3]

Today, however, upon completion of graduate degrees or diploma programs in opera and voice, students are entering a market for which they are ill prepared—a market unlike that of their predecessors—in which standing still and singing is no longer sufficient. The current climate is one in which opera companies must compete for the consumers' ever-shrinking discretionary dollar. The arena of competitors includes television, theatre, film, musical theatre, and even opera itself (in the form of recorded media).

---

1. Peter Gelb, "The Future of Opera," [audio] (lecture, Chautauqua Institution, August 17, 2007), *The Great Lecture Library*, Chautauqua Institution, Chautauqua, NY.
2. Ibid.
3. Roger Savage, "Staging an Opera: Letters from the Caesarian Poet," *Early Music* 26 (1998): 584–585.

This competition is not limited, however, to other forms of entertainment. As is the case with most opera companies, the Metropolitan Opera is currently undertaking drastic cost-cutting measures in order to shore up budgetary deficiencies. In short, there is more competition for less work.

The aging of the reliable audience is also of great concern for opera administrators. Gelb, in his lecture, mentioned that the average age of the Met's audience had gone from sixty to sixty-five over a recent five-year period. An article in *Vanity Fair* on the subject of the Met's budgetary issues put the national average age of operagoers at forty-eight. The building of a youthful audience, understandably, has become a focus of marketing and development departments around the country.

The canceling of productions in addition to new competition from other forms of entertainment requires young singers to become more skilled in order to work; singers are expected to have more than just a beautiful voice. Young professionals entering the work force are now required to possess skills in the areas of dance and movement, stage combat, and most importantly and most often neglected, acting. Singers, specifically young singers, spend endless hours working on their musical craft and vocal technique, but few seek or are offered the theatrical training necessary to compete in the ever-changing world of professional opera.

Whereas theatrical conservatories typically espouse specific philosophies or models by which they teach their craft (e.g., Stanislavski, Strasberg, Meisner, Hagen, or Adler techniques), operatic performers have not had such a dedicated system by which to study or prepare arias, scenes, or entire roles dramatically. Though acting will likely never replace singing as the primary area of focus in opera, singers longing for careers in opera will be judged not only as singers, but as total performers. The mining of existing acting techniques for those tenets applicable to and sustainable in opera, and the application of these concepts to a systematic analysis of the libretto, can present an effective model for training singers, thus preparing them for the realities that they will face in the new professional environment.

PART I

BACKGROUND

CHAPTER ONE

An Argument for Opera as a Theatrical Art Form

As mentioned earlier, a director for whom I served as assistant director once commented that he felt the music was more important than the drama—meaning the acting—in opera. This may be evidence of a largely held opinion that opera is a musical, not theatrical, art form—a seemingly innocent but important distinction. This philosophy can likely be traced to the rise of the superstar singer, the replacement of the producer with that of the conductor in terms of operatic production import, and even recorded media. Consider the operas collectively known as *bel canto*, which literally means "beautiful singing." Bel canto repertoire was marked by an increased importance in the technique of singing and a move away from storytelling.

The hierarchy of operatic staffs has also changed considerably since opera's inception. There are many more conductors who hold the position of artistic director than there are stage directors (what was once the producer). Whereas producers of old would concern themselves with the production as a whole, conductors (even as artistic directors) are typically (and understandably, to a degree) more interested in the music.

Historically, however, there is significant evidence that opera was first conceived as a theatrical art form that employed music to enhance the emotional experience. At the very least, opera was meant to have parity between its major components. Writings throughout history show that opera was and is meant to be a true fusion of art forms in which no element is more important than the other. Donald J. Grout, the great music historian from whose books most musicians learned music history, identifies opera in two categories: one in which the music and drama or theatre are of equal import, and the second which he refers to as "singer's opera"—those operas in which the libretto is only a conveyance for beautiful singing and beautiful music.[1] In this second category, Grout goes so far as to mention the operas of specific composers including Rossini, Bellini, Verdi, and "most Italian composers." However, Verdi's inclusion in this group may be argued. His own letters provide evidence that he felt at least somewhat differently (as will be illuminated in later chapters).

In modern American politics, constitutional arguments are often framed in the context of what the "founding fathers intended." As for opera, one need only look to the writings of members of the Florentine Camerata to see what the "founding fathers" of opera were attempting to create. It is first necessary, however, to understand the artistic and musical climate that gave rise to the art form itself.

Opera's inception is credited to two groups, the first of which was a collection of philosophers, musicians, and writers who met in Florence between approximately 1573 and 1587. The central figure of this group was Count Giovanni de' Bardi in whose court the group met. Bardi was a nobleman who was educated in Greek and Latin and had served in the military defending the island of Malta against the Ottoman Empire. In later life, Bardi was called to Rome to serve Pope Clement VIII. However, it was the period between his military career and his service to the Pope that had a most profound impact on the direction of music and theatre.

Bardi was a great patron of the arts, especially music, employing such notable musicians as Vincenzo Galilei and Giulio Caccini (Pietro Strozzi was the third musician associated with the Camerata). Around 1572, Galilei and Bardi became interested in the writings of Girolamo Mei, an expert on Greek music and literature. It is this relationship that changed the direction of music in the eyes of Bardi and set in motion the events that led to opera as an art form.[2] During the wedding of Ferdinando de' Medici to Christine of Lorraine in 1589, Bardi organized entertainment that included a comedy by Girolamo Bargagli, *La pellegrina*. The *intermedi*[3] for this comedy included a work considered the predecessor to *Dafne*, the first true opera. This piece, a telling of Apollo and his slaying of the dragon Python, was performed to great acclaim by Jacopo Peri, a singer of great reputation and the future composer of *Dafne*.[4]

By 1592, Galilei and Caccini were experimenting with a style of singing

---

1. Donald J. Grout, *A Short History of Opera*, 3rd ed. (New York: Columbia University Press, 1988), 7.

2. *Grove Music Online*, "Bardi, Giovanni de', Count of Vernio," by Claude V. Palisca, accessed May 7, 2010, http://www.oxfordmusiconline.com/subscriber/article/grove/music/02033.

3. *Intermedi* (or *intermezzi*) were musical performances that occurred between the acts of plays.

4. Stanley Sadie, *History of Opera* (New York: W. W. Norton, 1990), 15.

reminiscent of that likely used in Greek tragedy. Caccini would describe this style of vocal music as "speaking in melody." C. V. Palisca describes additional principles laid out by the members of the Camerata:

> The ancient tonoi should be imitated, because they allow the affections of the texts to be expressed by the appropriate range of the voice; only one melody should be sung at one time, counterpoint being useful only for assuring fullness of harmony in the accompaniment; and the rhythm and melody should follow carefully the manner and speaking voice of someone possessed of a certain affection.[5]

It is this last item that is particularly germane to this book.

By 1592, Bardi had moved to Rome to serve the Pope, and the job of creating opera fell to a second group (also referred to occasionally as the Camerata), anchored by Jacopo Corsi. Though there was overlap in the membership of these two groups (namely, Caccini), it is Corsi's stewardship and not Bardi's that ultimately led to the creation of what are widely considered the earliest operas—*Dafne* in 1598 and *Euridice* in 1600.[6]

It is likely that the creators of opera envisioned an art form more equal in its nature. It was Greek drama, specifically tragedy, that the creators of opera found intriguing. The Camerata's aim was to return to the purity of the music of ancient Greece, intrigued specifically by the fact that Greek drama was sung or spoken in a highly emotionally charged manner.[7] As Greek drama was a vehicle for theatrical storytelling rather than musical delivery, it is fair to assume that the Camerata's interest in creating opera was, at the very least, fueled by an interest in dramatic forms as well as Greek music theory. Evidence of the Camerata's intent may be found in the dedication of Ottavio Rinuccini's libretto for Peri's *Euridice* to Maria de' Medici, the Queen of France: "It has been the opinion of many, Most Christian Queen, that the tragedies put on the stage by the ancient Greeks and Romans were sung throughout."[8] Caccini's dedication of his version of *Euridice* to Bardi puts forth a similar idea: "And this, too, is the manner which, in the years when your Camerata flourished in Florence, you and many other noble

---

5. Claude V. Palisca, "Camerata," in *Grove Music Online, Oxford Music Online* (accessed May 17, 2010); available from http://www.oxfordmusiconline.com:80/subscriber/article/grove/music/04652.
6. Ibid.
7. Paul Griffiths and Nicholas Temperley, "Opera," *The Oxford Companion to Music*, ed. Allison Latham, (Oxford: Oxford University Press, 2002), 863.
8. Piero Weiss, *Opera: A History in Documents* (New York: Oxford University Press, 2002), 12.

connoisseurs asserted the ancient Greeks used in performing their tragedies and other fables employing song."[9]

It is a commonly held belief that Greek bards passed on tales and fables through song. In this case, music was simply the conveyance for the telling of stories. Homer, credited as the author of *The Iliad* and *The Odyssey*, was himself a singer who passed on these tales through song (only to be committed to paper centuries later). Some modern scholars have even moved away from the belief that a single man named "Homer" actually existed. Rather, there is a theory that "Homer" was a collection of singers. Why is this evidence germane to the discussion of opera? It would seem that in ancient Greece, music (especially song) and drama were inextricably connected, and music was an important component in storytelling. In *Poetics*, Aristotle goes so far as to define *tragedy* as "an imitation of some action that is important, entire, and of a proper magnitude—by language, embellished and rendered pleasurable."[10] Aristotle further defines "pleasurable language" as "language that has the embellishments of rhythm, melody, and metre"[11]—a distinct reference to the art of singing.

If we are to believe the letters and dedications of the creators of the operatic form, we must assume that drama was of equal import or, more controversially, more important than the music. As is the case with most art forms, opera's formula was tampered with almost immediately. In his "reform operas," Christoph Willibald Gluck decried the direction opera had taken since its inception. The reform operas were meant to be a renaissance of the classical ideals, a return to the influence of the ancient Greeks—the same philosophy that led to opera's creation.

Despite a rather clear and documented intent delivered through history by opera's creators, between 1598 and today, drama, theatre, and acting have lost their significance in opera. In the next chapter, the path of drama in opera versus that of theatre will be examined.

---

9. Ibid., 17.
10. Thomas Twining, *Aristotle's Treatise on Poetry* (London: McDowall, 1815), 73.
11. Ibid.

CHAPTER TWO

A Brief History of Acting Across Disciplines

Considered a "perfect" art form, opera creates a synergy of vocal and instrumental music, theatre, dance, costuming, properties (or "props"), as well as architecture and painting in the form of scenery. In his book *A History of Opera: Milestones and Metamorphoses*, Burton Fisher describes opera in the following manner:

> In its most ideal and literal form, opera is sung drama, or music drama. Words performed with music can express what language alone has exhausted, a combination that achieves an expressive and emotive intensity that neither words nor music can achieve alone. Opera unites those two expressive languages into its art form; at times it is sung speech, whose dramatic essence derives from music's intrinsic power to transcend words and heighten, arouse, and intensify emotions.[1]

A survey of multiple sources reveals striking similarities between definitions of the term *opera* with respect to drama. *The Harvard Dictionary of Music*, for example, defines *opera* as "drama that is primarily sung, accompanied by instruments, and presented theatrically."[2] Further sources, ranging from academic to commonplace, describe *opera* as "a drama set to music to be sung with instrumental accompaniment by singers usually in costume,"[3] "a drama in which actors sing throughout,"[4] or finally, "a drama in which the characters sing, rather than speak, all or most of their lines. Opera is one of the most complex of all art forms. It combines acting, singing, orchestral music, costumes, scenery, and often ballet or some other form of dance."[5]

---

1. Burton D. Fisher, *A History of Opera: Milestones and Metamorphoses* (Miami: Opera Journeys, 2005), 14.
2. *Harvard Dictionary of Music*, 4th ed. (Cambridge: Belknap, 2003)., s.v. "opera."
3. *Oxford Dictionary of Music*, 2nd ed. (Oxford University Press, 1994), s.v. "opera."
4. *New Grove Dictionary of Music and Musicians*, 2nd ed. (London: Macmillan 2001), s.v. "opera."
5. *World Book Encyclopedia*, s.v. "opera."

A common element in most if not all definitions and histories of opera is the use of the terms *acting* or *drama* and the idea that opera is meant to be, by its very nature, "presented theatrically." Also striking is the use of the term *actors* in the defining phrase "actors sing throughout," rather than "singers sing throughout." This distinction seems to challenge the widely held opinion that opera singers and actors have different goals.

Further evidence of drama's import as an element of opera may be seen when considering the distinction drawn between opera and oratorio. *Oratorio* is defined as "a dramatic musical composition for singers. Most oratorios are based on religious stories. They are performed by soloists, a chorus, and an orchestra without acting, costumes, or scenery."[6]

It would seem that operatic and theatrical acting were once on a parallel course when considering the gesture- and pose-based presentation that dominated operatic acting and is still found in some modern productions (though what exists today is reserved primarily for the "stylization"[7] of productions).[8] Acting prior to the twentieth century may be characterized by the use of "gesture," as defined and espoused by such figures as Gilbert Austin, Johannes Jelgerhuis, and François Delsarte. Austin's *Chironomia* illustrated and defined the body language of what was known as "rhetorical delivery" (illustrations 2.1, 2.2, and 2.3). Johannes Jelgerhuis's treatise *Theoretische lessen over de gesticulatie en mimiek* (Theoretical Lessons Concerning Gesture and Facial Expressions) described facial gestures and their related emotional expression (illustration 2.4). Yet the most significant early proponent of gesture and pose was François Delsarte, whose "Applied Aesthetics" were so widely accepted and popular during the nineteenth century that singers and actors alike credited Delsarte as critical to their successes on the dramatic and operatic stages.[9]

---

6. *World Book Encyclopedia*, s.v. "oratorio."

7. The "stylized" production is one that often follows a specific style of acting or visual theatre. Elia Kazan described stylization in the following fashion: "Stylized acting and direction is to realistic acting and direction as poetry is to prose" (Elia Kazan, *Kazan on Directing* [Vintage: New York, 2010], 46.). In other words, a "stylized" production is any production that uses as its concept "old" or invented styles of presentation. Robert Wilson's operatic direction has often been described as stylized.

8. Charles Isherwood, "Operatic Acting? Oxymoron No More," *New York Times*, September 9, 2007.

9. Richard G. King, "How to be an Emperor: Acting Alexander the Great in Opera Seria," *Early Music* 36 (2008), 181–202; Nancy Lee Chalfa Ruyter, *The Cultivation of Body and Mind in Nineteenth-Century American Delsartism* (Westport: Greenwood, 1999), 13.

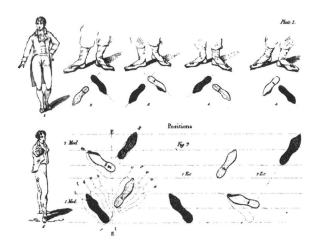

Illustration 2.1: Examples of Gilbert Austin's "Positions of the Feet and Lower Limbs" (Austin, 1806, pl.1).

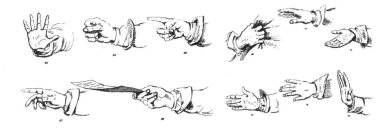

Illustration 2.2: "Positions of the Hands Used by Ancient Orators" (Austin, 1806, pl.7).

Illustration 2.3: Examples of Gilbert Austin's "Complex Significant Gestures" (Austin, 1806, pl.12). This particular plate shows an example of how gestures may be assigned to preexisting material.

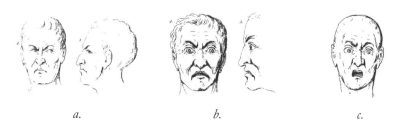

a.   *b.*   *c.*

Illustration 2.4: Facial gestures (Jelgerhuis, 1927), showing: a. contempt (pl.38), b. anger (pl. 32), and c. fright (pl. 34).

FRANÇOIS ALEXANDRE NICOLAS CHÉRI DELSARTE

François Alexandre Nicolas Chéri Delsarte was born in France in 1811 and died in 1871. After a brief stint as an art student, Delsarte studied singing at the Paris Conservatoire and was, for a brief time, on the roster of the Opéra-Comique. Delsarte, however, is best known for his "Applied Aesthetics"[10]—a theatrical Rosetta Stone meant to provide actors and singers with a palette of positions and gestures from which they could choose, depending on the emotion that they wanted to convey. Delsarte formed his theories based on extensive observations, which he then organized into a system. In the following excerpt, Delsarte describes one such observation:

> I noticed, in fact, that in all these corpses the thumb displayed a similar tendency,—that of adduction or attraction inward. Now I prove that the thumbs of the dying man contracted at first in an almost imperceptible degree . . . Thus, I had acquired the proof that not only does the adduction of the thumb characterize death, but that this phenomenon indicates the approach of death in proportion to its intensity.[11]

Upon completion of such observations, Delsarte began to apply them to human emotional expression (thus the term "Applied Aesthetics") and, by relation, to acting. The following is an example found in Genevieve Stebbins's *Delsarte System of Expression*. Delsarte's functions of the hand, as illuminated by Stebbins, are "to define or indicate, to affirm or deny, to mold or detect, to conceal or reveal, to surrender or hold, to accept or reject, to inquire or acquire, to support or protect, and to caress or assail."[12] A description of the specifics of these functions is as follows:

---

10. Ruyter, *Cultivation*, 5; E. T. Kirby, "The Delsarte Method: 3 Frontiers of Actor Training," *The Drama Review: TDR* 16 (March 1972), 55.

11. Genevieve Stebbins, *Delsarte System of Expression* (New York: Werner, 1902), 177.

12. Ibid., 173–174.

Description of Movement

1. (a) To define: first finger prominent; hand moves up and down, side to earth.
   (b) To indicate: first finger prominent; hand points to the object to be indicated.
2. (a) To affirm: hand, palm down, makes movement of affirmation up and down.
   (b) To deny: hand, palm down, makes movement of negation from side to side.
3. (a) To mold: hand makes movement as if molding a soft substance, as clay.
   (b) To detect: rub the thumb across the fingers as if feeling a texture held between them. (A movement often made when following a train of thought.)
4. (a) To conceal: bring the palm of the hand toward you, the fingers at the same time gently closing on palm.
   (b) To reveal: reverse the above movement, exposing the palm.
5. (a) To surrender: closed hand opens, palm down, action as if dropping something on the ground.
   (b) To hold: the hand closes as if to retain something.
6. (a) To accept: fingers close on upturned palm as if receiving something.
   (b) To reject: fingers unclose from a downturned palm as if throwing something away.
7. (a) To inquire: a tremulous movement of the outstretched fingers as in the blind; palm down.
   (b) To acquire: hand drawn toward you, fingers curve toward down-turned palm.
8. (a) To support: palm up, making a flat surface as if supporting a weight.
   (b) To protect: palm down; a movement of fingers as if covering what you protect.
9. (a) To caress: a movement of stroking up and down, or sideways. If sideways, one caresses the animal nature.
   (b) To assail: palm down; the fingers make a convulsive movement of clutching.[13]

Such movements were then modified by what Delsarte referred to as "attitudes" creating a palate of positions coinciding with various emotional

---

13. Ibid., 174–175.

states. The following illustration shows three hand positions relating to open, closed, and forced (*Normo, Concentro,* and *Excentro,* respectively) each divided into three attitudes (concentric, normal, excentric) equaling nine different emotional states.[14]

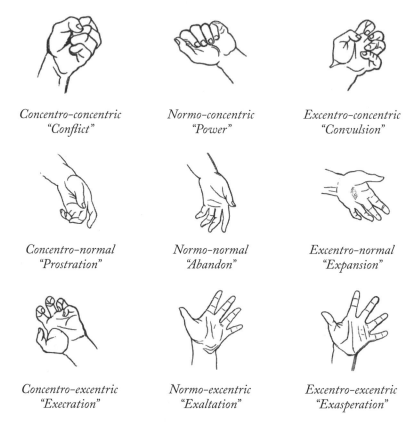

Concentro-concentric	Normo-concentric	Excentro-concentric
"Conflict"	*"Power"*	*"Convulsion"*

Concentro-normal	Normo-normal	Excentro-normal
"Prostration"	*"Abandon"*	*"Expansion"*

Concentro-excentric	Normo-excentric	Excentro-excentric
"Execration"	*"Exaltation"*	*"Exasperation"*

Illustration 2.5: Illustrations of Delsarte's "Conditional Attitudes of the Hand" (Stebbins, 1902, 181) with corresponding descriptions of the emotional results (Delaumosne et. al., 1887, 475).

Despite the popularity that organizational systems such as that of Delsarte enjoyed throughout the nineteenth century, by the early twentieth century, a movement was afoot in the theatre toward realism onstage. Of this phenomenon, director Edwin Duerr wrote, "By the close of the nineteenth century the majority of actors decided perforce to be more real than theatrical onstage, to be more representational."[15] Though theatrical training

---

14. L'Abbé Delaumosne, Angélique Arnaud, François Delsarte, Frances A. Shaw, and Abby Langdon Alger, *Delsarte System of Oratory* (New York: Werner, 1887), 472–475.

15. Edwin Duerr, *The Length and Depth of Acting* (New York: Holt, Rinehart and Winston, 1962), 404.

began to move away from gesture and pose, the fact that operatic acting remained married to a *presentational* approach (rather than *representational*) is evidenced by articles and treatises on the subject.

It is important, before further discussion of this move, to define and distinguish between presentational and representational with regard to acting. There are two schools of thought on the terms *representational* and *presentational* as they relate to acting technique. Representational acting is defined by Uta Hagen as "to imitate or illustrate the character's behavior," whereas the "presentational actor attempts to reveal human behavior through a use of himself, through an understanding of himself and consequently an understanding of the character he is portraying."[16] This interpretation stems directly from Stanislavski, who used *presentational* to describe the favorable acting technique. However, a more accepted classification today would be the opposite. Robert Blumenfeld defines presentational acting as "the old-fashioned, external, technical, non-organic approach to acting, in which the character is 'presented' or shown to the audience by the actor, who does not feel any of the character's emotions, but rather imitates, simulates, or counterfeits them."[17] By contrast, Blumenfeld defines representational acting as "contemporary acting practice, in which the actor 'represents' the character by living through the character's life moment to moment."[18] To alleviate confusion, for the purposes of this discussion, Blumenfeld's definitions will be used.

An article published during the maturation and spread of modern acting technique, and entitled "The Technique of Operatic Acting," not only extols the virtues of gesture as a means of conveying emotional ideas, but advocates "posing" in the delivery of operatic ideas.

> The presentation of such a drama, the task of communicating a world of inner conflict and emotion directly to the heart of the listener, will naturally demand a certain technique of its own, in general a technique of large lines, which will make as nearly as possible exhaustive use of the pose, and of that variation of the pose which consists in sustaining a comparatively motionless bodily attitude, if effective, throughout a whole scene, even while singing. It is a technique, in short, which strives to eliminate all ineffective outer gestures and to produce a maximum of expression with the simplest means, preeminently with utilization of sustained attitudes

16. Uta Hagen, *Respect for Acting* (New York: Wiley, 1973), 11–12.
17. Robert Blumenfeld, *Blumenfeld's Dictionary of Acting and Show Business* (New York: Limelight Editions, 2009), 210.
18. Ibid., 231.

of the body, among which the dramatic use of the eyes, the deliberately sustained gaze, is perhaps the most important subdivision. Another variation is the *moving* pose, composed of a fixed gaze, shoulders and body as nearly motionless as possible, and a scarcely perceptible, sliding motion of the feet which will suffice, nevertheless, to carry the actor clear across the stage if desired, without breaking the pose, the impression of which is after all invariably centered in the eyes.[19]

In addition to the simplification of building a character, another perceived benefit to gesture- and pose-based acting was the use of what might be called "character templates" when preparing roles:

> This formal, highly codified acting technique made the singer's job easier. Once learned, the gestures could be used again and again. The performer would have "acted" them all before, often to the same text (for example, in settings of Metastasio's librettos), or even to the same text and music (in the case of baggage arias).[20]

It is likely, despite the popularity of gesture and pose as a means of acting in the eighteenth and nineteenth centuries, that a more representational style of acting did exist. Denis Diderot (1713–84) was one of the first to recognize that there were two schools of thought with regard to acting on stage: the first, the outward or presentational approach, in which the actor remained removed emotionally from his or her character; and the second, that of "emotional involvement," in which the actor became intimately connected to the character that he or she was portraying (or a representational style). Diderot's analysis of acting (as was the case with most of his contemporaries and some modern operatic critics) arrived at the conclusion that an actor steeped in the emotion of the character would be inconsistent, unpredictable, and unable to communicate effectively and coherently with his or her audience.[21] To Diderot, the perfect actor must be emotionally as "an unmoved and disinterested onlooker" with "penetration and no sensibility."[22] It was Delsarte who codified Diderot's analysis into a system. However, in an attempt to introduce a system that would lead to a more organic and less mechanical approach than that of his predecessors,

---

19. Bennett Challis, "The Technique of Operatic Acting," *The Musical Quarterly* 13 (1927), 633–634.

20. King, "Emperor," 184.

21. Daniel Meyer-Dinkgräfe, *Approaches to Acting: Past and Present* (New York: Continuum, 2005), 29.

22. Ibid.

Delsarte succeeded only in creating a system that led to a disconnect between character and actor.[23]

CONSTANTIN SERGEYEVICH ALEKSEIEV STANISLAVSKI

Opera and theatre seemed to be on parallel paths with regard to acting for most of operatic history—there was no significant distinction made between operatic acting and theatrical acting.[24] The divergence of the two disciplines likely occurred in the early 1900s with the popularization of a system of acting developed by Constantin Sergeyevich Alekseiev Stanislavski (a.k.a. Konstantin Stanislavsky).[25] It may have been, in fact, the techniques of Delsarte, his contemporaries, and those who would continue to espouse their practices that Stanislavski, long considered the father of Method acting, rebelled against in creating his technique and subsequent teaching system.

Modern acting technique has been attributed largely to Stanislavski and his progeny—most notably, Lee Strasberg, Uta Hagen, Sanford Meisner, and Stella Adler. Stanislavski's work began in the late nineteenth century and was largely based on a philosophy of representation rather than presentation (note the earlier discussion on the use of these terms).

Understanding the system created by Constantin Stanislavski begins with an understanding of his creative crisis, which brought about the system's conception. As is common with roles that are repeated many times (and is especially true in opera, as singers often make entire careers out of singing the same roles over and over), Stanislavski found that a role for which he had accumulated a great deal of acclaim had become routine. He had arrived at a point of simply going through the motions.[26] In *My Life in Art*, Stanislavski writes, "I had mechanically repeated these fixed appurtenances of the role and the physical signs of absent emotion."[27] He felt himself beginning to *imitate* emotions rather than to *have* emotions. Once inspiration returned for the role (interestingly, not in performance or rehearsal but while he was

---

23. Lee Strasberg, "Acting," *Encyclopædia Britannica*, vol. 1 (Chicago: University of Chicago, 1978), 60.

24. Reinhard Strohm, *Dramma per musica: Italian Opera Seria of the Eighteenth Century* (New Haven: Yale University Press, 1997), 224.

25. A word about spelling: There are many references to *Constantin Stanislavski*, and depending on the source, it may be spelled in different ways (the most notable variation is *Konstantin Stanislavsky*). I have chosen the former, if for no other reason than that it was familiar to me. However, I have attempted to mitigate any confusion by following the author's spelling when footnoting or referencing other works.

26. Robert Blumenfeld, *Using the Stanislavsky System: A Practical Guide to Character Creation & Period Styles* (Limelight Editions: New York, 2008), 17.

27. Constantin Stanislavski, *My Life in Art* (New York: Routledge, 1987), 460, quoted in Blumenfeld, *Stanislavsky System*, 17.

on vacation), Stanislavski began to search for a way to find the freshness and connection to the character each time he stepped onto the stage to perform it. It was this quest that brought about Stanislavski's System, or what is more commonly known in the United States as his *Method* (from the *Method of Physical Action,* and thus the phrase Method acting).[28]

Though the greatest advancement in the study of acting is commonly attributed to Stanislavski's System, it was the prolific Russian actor Mikhail Semyonovich Shchepkin who first inspired Stanislavski and gave him "the basis upon which he was to build his 'system.'"[29] This basis can be found in the following principles of acting that governed Shchepkin's work:

1. For the gaining of truth in a role the actor can use life experience, observations, and imagination upon which to build. The actor should not try to wipe out his or her personality but rather use it advantageously for the role.
2. The actor makes a role consistently believable by concentrating upon the "through actions" of the character or upon his or her main drives, which can be found by a careful study of the script. He or she concentrates on these and the other actors rather than on the audience.
3. The actor must adhere to the script.
4. The actor strives for ensemble.
5. An actor must have technique, i.e., a flexible, expressive, and controlled voice and body with which to express the inner reality of his or her role.
6. An actor should play simply and naturally.
7. The actor should respect his or her work and colleagues in the theatre, always maintaining an individual discipline as well as helping contribute to a group discipline.[30]

Shchepkin, deemed by Stanislavski "the great artist and lawgiver of the Russian stage,"[31] was born into serfdom in 1788, eventually becoming a famous actor in his own right and the director of the Maly Theatre in Moscow. It was the Maly at which Shchepkin imparted his philosophy that acting was based in realism, rather than the gesture and pose ideal espoused

28. Ibid., 17.
29. Charles Metten, "Artist and Lawgiver of the Russian Stage," *Educational Theatre Journal* 14 (March 1962), 44.
30. Ibid., 48.
31. Konstantin Stanislavsky, *My Life in Art,* trans. J. J. Robbins (New York: Theatre Arts Books, 1948), 65, quoted in Metten, 44.

in the classical acting traditions and accepted by so many for so long.[32] Like Stanislavski, Shchepkin was also inspired unexpectedly by another actor. Shchepkin first became enamored with the idea of realism on stage when profoundly moved at a performance by Prince Mestchersky in 1810. Of this performance, Shchepkin wrote:

> I fell under the spell of real life, and it did not release its hold on me till the end of the performance. I saw no one on the stage except the Prince. My eyes seemed to have become glued to him. His suffering struck a living chord in my soul; every word delighted me by its naturalness and at the same time tormented me.[33]

Shchepkin changed his attitude toward the stage and began to strive for a more realistic and truthful approach in his own acting. He attempted to find himself in the characters he played rather than attempting to *become* someone else (a philosophy that Stanislavski advocated in his work and in his teaching).[34]

Though he died in the year of Stanislavski's birth, Shchepkin's letters and his mentorships of certain students allowed for his influence to extend to Stanislavski some years later. Two of Shchepkin's contemporaries and actors from the Maly Theatre, Alexander Fedotov and Glikeria Fedotova, worked with Stanislavski, directing him and critiquing some of his early work (respectively).[35]

STANISLAVSKI AND SCIENCE

Stanislavski's ideas were revolutionary not only in the realm of the theatre, but also as related to the burgeoning field of psychology. Through his work flowed one truth that would be difficult to debate—physical action requires psychological stimulus, and psychological desires require physical action to be realized. Was there a scientific influence governing Stanislavski, or was this coincidence? Did he follow the theories of Freud or Pavlov? It may be beneficial, at this point, to deal with these questions, as they tend to cloud the perception of his actual work, and for the purposes of the singer are extraneous.

In his book *Science and the Stanislavsky Tradition of Acting*, Jonathan Pitches illuminates the conflict within Stanislavski himself on the subject of science.

---

32. Metten, 46.
33. David Magarshack, *Stanislavsky, A Life* (New York: Chanticleer, 1951), 140.
34. Metten, 46.
35. Blumenfeld, *Stanislavsky System*, 13.

If you were to take Stanislavsky at his word, any search for a scientific root to the tradition of acting associated with his name would be futile. His preface to *An Actor's Work on Himself* (1938) is unequivocal: "Do not look for any scholarly or scientific derivations. We in the theatre have our own lexicon, our actors' jargon which has been wrought out of life."[36]

Despite Stanislavski's professions to the contrary, Pitches draws attention to the fact that Stanislavski was of two minds on the subject of science, and seemed to contradict himself even within the same text—*An Actor's Work on Himself.*[37]

In the chapter "Some Conclusions on Acting," Stanislavsky casts himself in the role of scientist, planting in the mind of the reader a set of persuasive relationships between his System and the discipline of science—rigour, clarity, objectivity, experimentation—and allying them with his own project.[38]

Whether or not Stanislavski's work in the theatre was science or scientific, his process of drawing inner feelings to the surface as a tool for creation shares many traits with psychology. It was, after all, around the time that Stanislavski was to bring his System to bear on the theatre that Sigmund Freud was conveying his theories of "Psychoanalysis,"[39] and a full three decades before Abraham Maslow published *A Theory of Human Motivation* containing his well-known "Hierarchy of Needs."[40] Stanislavski's System has even shared common themes with many behavioral theories of modern psychologists. In their article "Stanislavski's Acting Method and Control Theory: Commonalities across Time, Place, and Field," Dyer P. Bilgrave and Robert H. Deluty describe the Stanislavski method as

a highly articulated and practical system of acting [that] presents a model of human behavior and motivation that is strikingly similar to the "control theory" of psychologists Charles Carver and Michael Scheier. These similarities are in the areas of (a) the regulation of behavior by goals, (b) the process of goal formation, (c) the hierarchical organization of behavior, (d) the disruption of goals by obstacles, (e) outcome expectancies, (f) the

---

36. Jonathan Pitches, *Science and the Stanislavsky Tradition of Acting* (New York: Routledge, 2006), 1.

37. *An Actor's Work on Himself* was published in the United States as *Building a Character.*
38. Pitches, 11.

39. Sigmund Freud, James Strachey, Anna Freud, and Carrie Lee, *Sigmund Freud; The Standard Edition of the Complete Psychological Works of Sigmund Freud* (Hogarth: London, 1955), 3.

40. Abraham Maslow, "A Theory of Human Motivation," in *Twentieth Century Psychology: Recent Developments in Psychology*, ed. Philip Harriman (New York: Philosophical Library, 1946), 22.

sequencing of behavior into units, and (g) the formation of identity.[41]

As Stanislavski's work has drawn comparisons to scientists such as Freud, Pavlov, and even Sir Isaac Newton, it is most likely that the work of Théodule Ribot was most influential with regard to Stanislavski's work. Ribot's *La Psychologie des Sentiments* (1896; published in Russia in 1906), which Stanislavski read in 1909, is the first known reference to one of the main tenets of Stanislavski's early work, "affective memory,"[42] a term most proponents of Method acting know well and which will be discussed in more detail in coming chapters.

The fact that Stanislavski identified certain elements as essential to human behavior long before many psychologists had classified them is extraordinary. Stanislavski's observations about human nature were simple yet profound, especially when considering that his intention was not to analyze human behavior as a tool of science or health. Rather, his goal was to achieve a character portrayal that stemmed from emotional realism with the same freshness in each and every performance.[43] It was some eighty years after Stanislavski created his System based on his understanding of human behavior that psychologists Charles S. Carver and Michael F. Scheier articulated strikingly similar ideas: "Human life is a continual process of establishing goals and intentions and adjusting current patterns of behavior so as to more closely match these goals."[44]

STANISLAVSKI AND THE OPERA STUDIO

As he had done for actors at the Moscow Art Theatre, Stanislavski created a studio for opera singers (the Bolshoi Opera Studio), at which he and his students explored opera as drama. The productions given at his opera studio lacked what might be considered "high production values," as they were meant primarily as teaching tools. The singers came predominantly from the Moscow Conservatory and performed in casual clothing with little or no scenery, accompanied by piano, in a room in Stanislavski's house. However, these productions were extraordinarily acted, uncut versions of operas typically produced in larger venues. The focus of Stanislavski's work was the marriage of truthful acting and

---

41. Dyer P. Bilgrave, and Robert H. Deluty, "Stanislavski Acting Method and Control Theory: Commonalities across Time, Place, and Field," *Social Behavior and Society* 32 (2004), 329–340.
42. Pitches, 91.
43. Blumenfeld, *Stanislavsky System*, 17.
44. Michael F. Scheier and Charles S. Carver, "A Model of Behavioral Self-Regulation: Translating Intention into Action," in *Advances in Experimental Social Psychology*, vol. 21, ed. Leonard Berkowitz (San Diego: Academic Press, 1988), 308.

musical interpretation, while the rest of the operatic profession was continuing on a path of beautiful singing and gesture- and pose-based acting.[45]

STANISLAVSKI'S INFLUENCE ON AMERICAN ACTING TRAINING

Though little is known of his success with singers, Stanislavski's work as a theatre teacher spawned many great actors and many schools of thought, all striving toward the same ideal. Among the practitioners and, ultimately, carriers of the acting torch were Uta Hagen (whose techniques are taught at HB Studio in New York City), Sanford Meisner (whose work is the primary basis for all acting instruction at the American Academy of Dramatic Arts and the Neighborhood Playhouse), Stella Adler (whose work is the basis for the Stella Adler Conservatory), and finally and perhaps most significantly, Lee Strasberg, whose work is the basis for instruction at the Lee Strasberg Theatre and Film Institute. Strasberg's most important contributions likely came during his years as the artistic director of the Actors Studio, an organization of actors, directors, and playwrights devoted to the teaching of Method acting. From 1949 until his death, Strasberg mentored such actors as Paul Newman, Al Pacino, Marilyn Monroe, Jane Fonda, James Dean, Dustin Hoffman, Eli Wallach, Robert DeNiro, Jack Nicholson, Ellen Burstyn, Steve McQueen, and Martin Landau, to name only a few.[46] In addition to the Strasberg Institute, his interpretation of Stanislavski's System is also the basis of current instruction at the Actors Studio Drama School at Pace University. As the Actors Studio grew, Strasberg parted with his mentor; while Stanislavski moved to refine his Method, Strasberg remained committed to Stanislavski's earlier teachings.

The American Academy of Dramatic Arts may provide the strongest evidence of the theatre's move away from Delsarte's gesture- and pose-based methods toward more Stanislavskian practices. The first training school for actors in the United States, the American Academy of Dramatic Arts (first called the Lyceum Theatre School) was founded in 1884 in New York City. The school took much of its model from the Paris Conservatoire, and as at the Conservatoire, Delsarte's methods were the prominent mode of instruction. With little success or distinction to speak of, the Lyceum was renamed the American Academy of Dramatic Arts (AADA), the Delsartian approach of gestural acting was abandoned, and the theories of Stanislavski were adopted. Today, AADA's primary approach to instruction is that of Sanford Meisner,

---

45. Constantin Stanislavski and Pavel Rumyantsev, *Stanislavski on Opera*, trans. and ed. Elizabeth Reynolds Hapgood (New York: Theatre Arts Books, 1975), 46–47.

46. Louis Scheeder, "Strasberg's Method and the Ascendancy of American Acting" in *Training of the American Actor*, ed. Arthur Bartow (New York: Theatre Communications, 2006), 3–13.

and alums include Lauren Bacall, Peter Bergman, Grace Kelly, Robert Redford, Edward G. Robinson, and Spencer Tracy, to name only a few.[47]

This change in the theatrical direction (from imitation to emotional and psychological connection) may have contributed to the secondary position that acting took in opera. Stanislavski's work, and that of his progeny, requires much more investment (both mental and emotional) than that of Delsarte. Whereas a singer could simply memorize the Delsartian gestures and repeat them, truly representational acting requires constant discovery, or freshness, in each and every performance. It is believed that more focus placed on acting takes focus away from singing. This may, in fact, be the reason that acting in opera did not progress as theatrical acting did, and the focus of opera began to lean toward beautiful singing only.

GEORGE E. SHEA

The divergence of the two disciplines, operatic acting and theatrical acting, can be seen in illustration 2.6, taken from a 1915 book by George E. Shea entitled *Acting in Opera*. Shea's book provides a clear example of Delsarte's continued influence in opera. The gesture in this illustration, according to Shea, is meant to be held throughout a musical phrase, and all gestures must "fall [be completed] on one of the strong beats of the musical measure and on some

Illustration 2.6: An example drawn from Shea's *Acting In Opera* (Shea, 1915, 16).

culminating point of the musical phrase, either vocal, orchestral, or choral."[48] Illustration 2.6 shows a gesture that Shea describes as follows:

Here you sing the aria's first section, which is perhaps an Andante. Just as

---

47. Arthur Bartow, ed., *Training of the American Actor* (New York: Theatre Communications, 2006), xviii–xix.

48. George E. Shea, *Acting in Opera* (London: Schirmer, 1915), 12.

you are about to attack it, you advance your

A. right foot slightly, throwing your weight thereon, and at the same time gently raising and extending the right hand, palm downward and fingers a bit separated, on a level with the chest. This position may suffice for a whole musical phrase, or more, according to the sentiments expressed.[49]

Acting in Opera is a detailed classification system of operatic "positions," breaking each down into several sublevels, the most important of which are the classifications of "gesture" and "attitude." Shea, one of the first American opera singers to perform in French opera houses, obviously modeled his work after Delsarte, as evidenced by the use of gesture modification, or "attitudes." An example of how such "attitudes" were applied can be seen in illustration 2.7. The photograph shows a "Rigid-Arm Gesture" with a "Class II Attitude." The "Rigid-Arm" classification is self-explanatory, while the "Class II Attitude" is described by Shea as follows:

> Body inclined forward; head erect: Incline the body forward, the weight on the forward foot, the toes only of rear foot touching the ground, head erect. (Note that if the weight is between the two feet the attitude is less affirmative, or its import is modified, or it forms a transition—a bridge— between two distinctly formed and more definite postures.) This attitude expresses, according to the varying positions of the arms and hands, as well as of the varying facial expression, *Affirmation, Contradiction, Accusation, Reproach, Vehemence, Ardor;* also *Supplication,* and *Fear.*[50]

Illustration 2.7: An example of what Shea described as a "Rigid-Arm Gesture (Class II Attitude)."(Shea, 1915, 22a).

---

49. Ibid., 13.
50. Ibid., 39.

Shea's purpose in writing this book, as stated in his introduction, is as true today as it was in 1915: "Most vocal students who expect to become opera singers—many of them already well advanced musically and vocally—are ignorant of the principles and of the practice of acting."[51]

It is in the introduction to Shea's book, however, that the prevailing theory of the time is also articulated: "The combination of glance, attitude, gesture, walk and bearing, which forms an easy and effective 'stage presence,' is essential to the equipment of an operatic artist."[52]

WAGNER'S DRAMATIC RENAISSANCE

Whereas Stanislavski's System signaled a move away from Delsarte and Diderot in theatre, an earlier movement toward a more realistic acting style in opera may be attributed to Richard Wagner and his Bayreuth productions. Many years before Stanislavski began to develop his System, Wagner was a proponent of a more equally balanced operatic experience. Wagner's role in the revival of the dramatic focus in opera is illuminated in the *New Grove Dictionary of Music and Musicians*:

> The prototype of the modern director emerged, most obviously in the formidable presence of Richard Wagner, whose Bayreuth stagings of his operas in the late 1870s and early 80s pioneered a darkened auditorium, an orchestra hidden from view and a new, more "naturalistic" acting style, all of which further intensified the sense of audience involvement in the visual spectacle.[53]

Wagner felt that drama was at the very least as important as the music, if not more so. In the introduction to *Opera and Drama*, Wagner—musician, composer, and critic—states that he wrote the book for the purpose of proving that in opera, "a heretofore undreamt significance not only can, but must be given to Drama."[54]

OTHER FACTORS CONTRIBUTING TO THE DEMISE OF DRAMATIC IMPORT

Whereas the short-lived focus (or refocus) on drama may be attributed to Wagner, it is possible that its demise can be attributed to the rise of

---

51. Ibid., vii.
52. Ibid.
53. James R. Anthony, "Opera," in *The New Grove Dictionary of Music and Musicians*, vol. 18, ed. Stanley Sadie (London: Macmillan, 2001), 417.
54. Richard Wagner, *Opera and Drama*, trans. William Ashton Ellis (Lincoln: University of Nebraska, 1995), 20.

the sound recording and the phonograph. Whether or not singers of the early twentieth century were skilled actors, music and drama in opera were inseparable entities until the advent, mass production, and mass acquisition of recorded media. Before the phonograph and similar devices, the only way to *hear* an operatic performance was to *see* opera in a theatre—music and drama together. With the advent of recorded media—and more importantly, its mass distribution—drama was removed from the operatic experience. This may have devalued the contribution of the libretto to the music. Of recorded media, specifically the phonographic disc, the great philosopher, sociologist, and music historian, Theodor Adorno, wrote:

> It allows for the optimal presentation of music, enabling it to recapture some of the force and intensity that had been worn threadbare in the opera houses. Objectification, that is, a concentration on music as the true object of opera, may be linked to a perception that is comparable to reading, to the immersion in a text.[55]

Simply put, one can focus on the music devoid of theatre and spectacle. With the advent of recorded media, the balance of drama and music in opera shifted, and the spectacle no longer obscured musical analysis. Listeners could now focus on opera specifically as a musical art form.

Yet another major factor in the removal of dramatic emphasis from opera during the course of history may be the lack of a director-performer mentorship akin to the master-apprentice relationship in theatre. In *Science and the Stanislavsky Tradition of Acting*, Jonathan Pitches describes this relationship occurring between directors and actors, specifically in the Russian theatrical tradition from which the Method sprang. "Since the early 1900s and Stanislavsky's first experiments with the System, the deep-seated connection between director and actor, teacher and student in Russia is striking."[56] Such a relationship between director and singer has not existed in opera, at least since the era of the superstar singer, with the possible exception of conservatory or university training where the director is often also a professor. A relationship of this type often exists between singer and conductor, voice teacher, and even vocal coach. But too often, as most artistic directors are conductors and rehearsal periods are ten to fourteen days, the professional operatic stage director is a "hired gun" who has little time to form such a bond.

---

55. Theodor Adorno, "Opera and the Long-Playing Record," trans. Thomas Y. Levin, *October* 55 (1990), 64.
56. Pitches, 3.

No matter what the ultimate culprit, at some point in its history and despite brief revivals, opera's balance of music and drama became unbalanced, heavily weighted toward the music. Today, however, market factors and the competitive nature of the operatic career seem to be sparking a new dramatic renaissance and a new interest in the total performer—singer *and* actor. This renaissance requires a new focus on the training of singers as actors.

CHAPTER THREE

A New Model for Training Singers

One of the many definitions of *opera* states: "For a successful career in opera, a singer must have acting skills in addition to an outstanding voice. Most young singers who plan a career in opera take several years of acting lessons."[1] However, the reality is that most singers pursuing operatic careers spend very little time in acting classes. A survey of the curricula offered to master's degree students by universities in the United States shows a lack of acting training required or even offered to singers preparing for professional careers. Not only is this oversight dangerous to their marketability, it may also cultivate in singers the perception that acting training is not important—an opinion they will likely pass on to future students. The curricula analyzed for this chapter represent a cross-section of available training in the United States, from the highest echelon (from both public and private schools), the median, and the lower (predominately public or state universities). These choices were decidedly weighted toward the higher echelon, as the resources available to students at these schools is assumed to be greater than those of smaller music departments.

If, as noted in the above definition, one assumes that singers must receive significant training in acting, a glance at the curriculum through which a master's degree student must navigate in order to graduate illuminates the reality of operatic training. Of the classes required and offered to master's students (those students most likely to be on the cusp of a career in opera), one finds many classes in operatic literature, chamber music, and music history. However, there is rarely if ever specific mention of theatre or acting classes and no suggestion that these classes are recommended. Similarly, an examination of artist and performance diploma programs, programs designed more specifically for students preparing for performing careers and focusing primarily on the area of interest (in this case, opera), illustrates how the "dramatic" or "acting" skills are incorporated into most programs.

---

1. Bauman, "Opera," 790.

Within these programs, there can be found only a cursory mention of "Opera Workshop." This course is typically a "catch-all" course that is meant, in most cases, to be time devoted to the learning of what are unfortunately considered secondary skills—dance and movement, stage combat, and acting. In reality, and in most cases, time in these classes is devoted to opera scenes rehearsals or, in some cases, main stage production rehearsals rather than skill acquisition. Many school and conservatory directors use this course to circumvent the requirements for acting set forth by the National Association of Schools of Music.

This problem is not limited to colleges and universities. Conservatories fare similarly in this respect. The fact is that most major university degree programs require little if any acting training. Some degree programs require acting training only to let their graduates matriculate without ever taking an acting class. Though this training is supposed to occur in Opera Workshop, it rarely does, and those charged with teaching Opera Workshop often do not have the specific training in acting required to teach the class. Smaller universities often hire voice teachers instead of directors to teach Opera Workshop. Few of these voice teachers have professional experience either as a singer or as a director. Most have little to no training in acting. Some schools will hire acting teachers from theatre departments to teach acting. Though any exposure to acting training is good, often the singers and acting teachers speak different languages when it comes to the stage, and most actors have little to no experience with opera or working in foreign languages.

If, again, one assumes that singers should be trained in acting, "take several years of acting lessons," or that at the very least, performance majors should receive a more all-encompassing education, then a more successful curriculum for master's and certificate or diploma students may be found in tables 3.1 and 3.2.

Designed based on the master of fine arts (MFA) model used in many acting programs, this curriculum employs the structured study of necessary skills including language acquisition, diction, stage combat, movement and dance, audition skills, and most important to the current discussion, the acquisition of acting skill. This model also allows for the required classes (noted as "Required Core Classes") necessary for accreditation. Whereas most master's programs in music require only two years to complete, the additional coursework in this model requires a third year. As most young-artist programs are now seeking singers in their mid- to late-twenties, this third year would provide invaluable experience at no career cost to the singer.

Table 3.1

MM in Opera Performance

Year 1		Year 2		Year 3	
Semester 1	Semester 2	Semester 1	Semester 2	Semester 1	Semester 2
Italian Language (Intensive)	Italian Language (Intensive)	French Language (Intensive)	French Language (Intensive)	German Language (Intensive)	German Language (Intensive)
Italian Diction	Italian Opera: 1750–Present	French Diction	English Diction	German Diction	German Opera: Post 1900
Italian Opera: 1600–1750	Acting II	French Opera	20th Century or English Opera	German Opera: Pre-1900	Opera as Business
Acting I	Style: Bel Canto	Acting III	Acting IV	Acting V	
Stylized Movement	Vocal Coaching	Stage Combat	Ballroom Dance	Audition Class	Vocal Coaching
Vocal Coaching	Voice Lessons	Vocal Coaching	Vocal Coaching	Vocal Coaching	Voice Lessons
Voice Lessons	*Required Core Class	Voice Lessons	Voice Lessons	Voice Lessons	*Required Core Class
*Required Core Class	Opera Production: Bel Canto	*Required Core Class	*Required Core Class	*Required Core Class	Opera Production: Italian
Opera Production: Italian (Mozart)	Opera Production 2: English	Role Preparation	Opera Production: English	Opera Production: German	Opera Production 2: English
Scenes Program		Opera Production: French (utilizing stage combat such as Faust or Carmen)	Opera Production 2: French or Italian	Scenes Program	
		Scenes Program			

*"Required Core Class" refers to those classes required for accreditation and include music theory and music history courses among others.

Table 3.2

Artist Diploma in Opera

Year 1		Year 2		Year 3	
Semester 1	Semester 2	Semester 1	Semester 2	Semester 1	Semester 2
Italian Language (Intensive)	Italian Language (Intensive)	French Language (Intensive)	French (Intensive)	German Language (Intensive)	German Language (Intensive)
Italian Diction	Italian Opera: 1750–Present	French Diction	English Diction	German Diction	German Opera: Post 1900
Italian Opera: 1600–1750	Acting II	Musicology: French Opera	20th Century or English Opera	German Opera: Pre-1900	Opera as Business
Acting I	Style: Bel Canto	Acting III	Acting IV	Acting V	Vocal Coaching
Stylized Movement	Vocal Coaching	Stage Combat	Ballroom Dance	Audition Class	Voice Lessons
Vocal Coaching	Voice Lessons	Vocal Coaching	Vocal Coaching	Vocal Coaching	Opera Production
Voice Lessons	Opera Production	Voice Lessons	Voice Lessons	Voice Lessons	Opera Production 2: English
Opera Production	Opera Production 2: English	Role Preparation	Opera Production	Opera Production	
Scenes Program		Opera Production	Opera Production 2: French or Italian	Scenes Program	
		Opera Production: French (utilizing stage combat such as *Faust* or *Carmen*)			
		Scenes Program			

In addition to acting classes in five of six semesters, these curricula connect the study of language, history, performance practice, and stage craft through common themes (e.g., French, French diction, and French opera are studied together). Unlike most curricula, these steps would be taken in sequence with no deviation, and significant restrictions would be placed on the practice of "testing out" of classes. With regard to coursework, the curricula above also satisfy the dictates of accreditation set forth by the National Association of Schools of Music (NASM), which require, among other things, "advanced theatrical skills."[2]

As previously mentioned, most of the theatrical requirements for students in opera fall to the instructor of Opera Workshop. However, it is common knowledge among deans and department chairs at universities and conservatories that the addition of classes to curricula can be avoided by the creative wording of the Opera Workshop class description. Behind closed doors, department chairs will admit that they do not require acting classes for vocal performance and opera majors, and subvert the NASM requirement by wording Opera Workshop class descriptions to include acting, stage combat, movement, and other accreditation requirements. Sadly, the reality is that these sections, if they are actually covered, are not taught by professionals versed in acting technique. In some schools, Opera Workshop is not required, or required for so few hours that all of these items cannot be covered.

The term *Opera Workshop* is borrowed from a pre–World War II institution that provided additional training to singers after university. Herbert Graf, producer and teacher, described Opera Workshop as an "experimental opera theatre" meant to bridge the gap between "school training and engagements with major professional companies."[3] This role is currently filled by operatic young artist or resident artist programs.

POPULAR TEXTS ON THE SUBJECT OF OPERATIC ACTING

The lack of acting training in existing curricula may not be attributable only to a lack of deference. Whereas theatrical training methods have been honed to the point of establishing variations, operatic acting has not, to this date, been so organized as to present a coherent methodology that is easily followed. Operatic acting classes in most conservatories lack common threads or even common terminology. Evidence of this fact is found in the lack of texts deemed essential for the training of singers. The following is an

---

2. National Association of Schools of Music, *Handbook 2009–2010* (Reston: National Association of Schools of Music, 2008), 108.

3. Herbert Graf, *Opera for the People* (Minneapolis: University of Minnesota Press, 1951), 98.

annotated bibliography containing some of the more popular texts on the subject of acting and singing.

Balk, H. Wesley. *The Complete Singer-Actor: Training for Music Theater.* Minneapolis: University of Minnesota Press, 1985.

The benefit to this work is the series of exercises devoted to the improvement of the skills required for singers in the music theater discipline. Parts 1 and 2 of the book are devoted to the philosophy of the form and the skill sets required to be successful in the form (respectively).

Ostwald, David F. *Acting for Singers: Creating Believable Singing Characters.* Oxford: Oxford University Press, 2005.

There is little to no historical background offered as this book delves directly into the problem at hand. Each of the fourteen chapters is divided into subjects meant to help singers understand acting technique and apply it to their particular genre. For example, chapter 1, entitled "The Divine Marriage: Combining Believable Acting with Expressive Singing," has among its divisions "Acting Actions," "Acting Feelings," and "Human Behavior." The appendices offer a sort of "handbook" for working with acting technique. Ostwald's expertise is derived from his professional career as a stage and operatic director and teacher. Though Ostwald has some respectable credits both as a teacher and director, one may question the depth of his expertise, as there is little evidence he ever sang a role on stage (nor is he a singer). Nevertheless, this book provides a well-organized and easily searchable resource for the singing actor.

Goldovsky, Boris. *Bringing Opera to Life: Operatic Acting and Stage Direction.* New York: Appleton-Century-Crofts, 1968.

Goldovsky wrote this book to the opera director and the opera performer delving into specific situations, including particular opera arias and scenes. Goldovsky begins each chapter dealing with a specific facet of opera acting, and in subsequent pages, uses the operatic literature to illustrate his point (e.g., after the chapter "Developing the character," Goldovsky uses act 2 from *La traviata* as a case study). This book deals more generally with acting and is less technical than most other books on the subject. It does, however, deal more specifically with the inherent musical issues caused by acting (e.g., intonation, annunciation, tempos). Goldovsky's background is that of a conductor and pianist, not an opera singer or actor. However, Goldovsky did create the New England Opera Theatre and was head of the New England Conservatory's and Tanglewood's opera programs.

Stanislavski, Constantin and Pavel Rumyantsev. *Stanislavski on Opera.* Edited and translated by Elizabeth Reynolds Hapgood. New York: Theatre Arts Books, 1975.

This book is a diary of sorts written by a member of the Bolshoi Opera Theatre (which Stanislavski created and where he taught). The first chapter is a recapitulation of Stanislavski's teachings during his time at the Bolshoi, including quotations, remarks, and answers to questions posed by his students. *Stanislavski on Opera* gives the reader an insight into his thoughts about the art form and about sung theatre. The remaining chapters in the book are devoted to seven operas, most by Russian or Slavic composers. These chapters analyze the operas from Stanislavski's point of view, giving some historical background but dealing mostly with the application of his work to these particular shows. These chapters were also written during actual rehearsals. His specific thoughts were recorded, including statements he made that were meant to move the singers toward more appropriate acting choices.

Clark, Mark Ross. *Singing, Acting, and Movement in Opera: A Guide to Singer-getics.* Bloomington: Indiana University Press, 2002.

Divided into three sections (Preparation, Integration, and Application), this book devotes only eight pages to character analysis and ten pages to preparing a role for the operatic stage. The majority of this work focuses on peripheral issues such as alignment, facial expression, performance anxiety, operatic careers, and stretching. Some helpful information can be found in the appendix, including a stage manager's handbook and a discussion of stage combat.

Burgess, Thomas. *The Singing and Acting Handbook: Games and Exercises for the Performer.* New York: Routledge, 2000.

Divided into two sections, this book is a simplified study of the elements of sung theatre, including discussions of needed skills such as rhythm, understanding scores, and exercises designed to introduce young actors to the musical drama stage.

Two additional texts worth noting are Daniel Helfgot and William O. Beeman's *The Third Line: The Opera Performer as Interpreter* (New York: Schirmer Books, 1993) and, as previously discussed, George Shea's *Acting in Opera* (though the latter is more of a curiosity than anything else). Some of these texts are appropriate to varying degrees. However, most seem disorganized when it comes to the technique of acting, establishing little by way of a process.

PART II

AN ACTING PRIMER

CHAPTER FOUR

The Method of Physical Action

It should be no surprise to anyone familiar with acting that most discussions of acting in the twentieth century would center around Constantin Stanislavski. The sheer volume of text devoted to Stanislavski's work is overwhelming for those looking to understand it. Stanislavski has been dissected not only by other actors, directors, and teachers, but also by scientists, philosophers, and historians.

Strasberg's divergence, the volume of information on Stanislavski, and the additions and explanations provided by so-called practitioners of the Method contribute to the confusion many singers and actors feel when attempting to understand Stanislavski's work. The following chapters will be devoted to reducing the masses of information to the most important tenets of the Method as it pertains to singing and, specifically, opera. It is important for the singer to understand before proceeding that Stanislavski was not simply an actor, director, and teacher of acting. Stanislavski studied singing at the Bolshoi Opera, performed operetta, was a friend to composers and an opera director, and worked with opera singers in his own opera studio. Stanislavski saw singers and actors as working towards the same goals. When addressing a group of actors and singers, Stanislavski said,

> You are preparing to participate in a collective undertaking. What does that mean? It means that you must be welded into one collective whole and learn as a group to care for your common work. And to learn how to do this means that you will be re-educated both as a person and as an actor.[1]

Stanislavski's underlying beliefs with regard to opera can also be seen in his writings on the subject. "Concert music is pure music. By contrast, operatic

---

1. Constantin Stanislavski, *Stanislavski's Legacy*, ed. and trans. Elizabeth Reynolds Hapgood (London: Max Reinhardt, 1958), 36.

music is subject to theatrical rules . . . The whole point is to convert a concert in costume, which is what most operatic performances are nowadays, into a genuine, dramatic spectacle."[2]

As alluded to in chapter 2, Stanislavski had many followers who professed to be teaching his Method of Physical Action but were, in fact, teaching variations on the purest form of his work. This leads to much confusion among actors, not to mention singers, interested in improving their craft. It helps to look more closely at the chronology of the Method. As Stanislavski's work is the basis for most acting technique today, it is important to understand the variations and their origins.

The Method of Physical Action, or the Method (also referred to as the System), was adopted by the Moscow Art Theatre in the 1920s and was the culmination of Stanislavski's work to that point—but only to that point. Little known to most (save those who have studied the System's origins) is the fact that Stanislavski's initial work at the Moscow Art Theatre marked the *beginning* of the process and not the codified end.

Stanislavski's first book, *An Actor Prepares*, recorded only what he had discovered by the time it was published. Even then, it took a few years for the book to reach the United States, by which time Stanislavski was already challenging some of his own very important early findings, (e.g., *affective memory*, to be discussed later in this and subsequent chapters). *An Actor Prepares* may be considered a loose collection of theories, with a true system only occurring as a result of his second book, *Building a Character*. A much more concise and efficient system was codified in his final book, *Creating A Role*, which was actually penned by Elizabeth Reynolds Hapgood from notes that Stanislavski had given her. By this time, Stanislavski's original ideas had gone through several important revisions, and though he was only a few years from death, he had not finished revising his process. It was almost a quarter-century after his death that *Creating a Role* reached the United States. The process of translating Stanislavski's work and publishing it in America produced a pronounced lag between what Americans believed the System was and what Europeans believed.

There was also much disagreement between the so-called Stanislavskians in the States, some of which was due to the constantly evolving work being done in Moscow. The actors who had studied (directly or indirectly) with Stanislavski early in his teaching career and then brought those ideas to America found themselves (sometimes blissfully) ignorant of the innovations the master was undertaking.

---

2. Ibid., 42.

Though Lee Strasberg eventually gained the reputation of being the great American teacher of the System, Strasberg's understanding of Stanislavski's work was almost forty years out of date and only indirectly informed. Strasberg studied at the American Lab Theatre, an institute created by students of the Moscow Art Theatre who had immigrated to the United States for various reasons. Among those teachers were Richard Boleslavsky (widely credited with bringing the System to America), Maria Germanova, and Maria Ouspenskaya.

As students learned of the changes undergone in the System, some accepted them and some rejected them outright. One of the first and most important changes was a move away from affective memory or emotional memory toward a system of cause and effect. Early in Stanislavski's career, there was some concentration on affective memory, or the memory of emotions, as an inner stimulus for truth onstage. Later in his career, at the behest of Eugene Vakhtangov (one of Stanislavski's most trusted students), Stanislavski began to look for internal motivations for external physical actions (discussed in the chapter on objectives, obstacles, and actions).[3] Such a dramatic change could have been a "shot heard round the world" if not for the fact that many of his followers ignored the new direction, and chief among those dissenters was Lee Strasberg. In his book *Since Stanislavski and Vakhtangov: The Method as a System for Today's Actor*, Lawrence Parke discusses the splintering of the American Stanislavskians:

> When Stella Adler returned from her visit with Stanislavski in 1934 and told Mr. Strasberg and others at the Group Theatre (which was at the time considered the "Mecca" of "the Method") that Stanislavski had abandoned his extensive work theretofore with *emotional memory* (later to be called *affective memory* and *emotional recall* by some), Mr. Strasberg is reported to have said "I never will!"[4]

In fact, one perusing the background section of the Lee Strasberg Theatre and Film Institute website will find mention of "the Method approach taught by Lee Strasberg," but no mention of Stanislavski. The website goes on to state that Strasberg *created* the Method replete with a mention of affective memory. "The reputation of the Institute as the nation's premier acting school is rooted in Lee Strasberg's development of the Method in

3. Lawrence Parke, *Since Stanislavski and Vakhtangov: The Method as a System for Today's Actor* (Hollywood: Acting World Books, 1985), 3.
4. Ibid., 6.

the early 1930s . . . Its academic approach focuses on motivation, affective memories and character immersion in a quest for authenticity."[5]

In the following chapters, attention will be given to illuminating the purest ideals of the Method in an attempt to alleviate some of this confusion. Attention will be given to the most important of Stanislavski's ideas (and the ideas of others). These ideas will be explained in a way that singers will not only understand, but relate to. The first step is to answer the question "What is Method acting?"

As the term *Method acting* flows from the Method of Physical Action, understanding Method acting is to understand the Method itself. There are many pieces to the Method of Physical Action. In her book *Stanislavski's Legacy*, Elizabeth Reynolds Hapgood enlightens readers on the basics of the Method by assembling the most concisely worded descriptions from Stanislavski's own writings and thoughts. Firstly Hapgood breaks down the Method into propositions. The first of these propositions warns that there are no shortcuts to great acting. True reality on stage is achieved only when the actor is

(a) physically free, in control of free muscles; (b) his attention must be infinitely alert; (c) he must be able to listen and observe on the stage as he would in real life, that is to say be in contact with the person playing opposite him; (d) he must believe in everything that is happening on the stage that is related to the play.[6]

The second of these propositions requires of the actor "a true inner creative state on the stage" that allows him or her to do all that the character requires—psychologically and physically.[7] The second paragraph discusses specific needs of the actor. These elements are most often described by modern scholars and teachers as *relaxation, concentration*, and *public solitude.*

In all of the writings and descriptions of Stanislavski's work, there is often an effort to confuse what seems in the above paragraphs to be very clear. Studying these paragraphs illuminates the main themes of Stanislavski's work: physical relaxation, attention and concentration, imagination, and the ability to listen. Stanislavski said, "*A true inner creative state* on the stage,

---

5. "Our Background," the website of the Lee Strasberg Theatre and Film Institute, accessed April 10, 2010, http://strasberg.com/lstfi/index.php?option=com_content&view=article&id =201&Itemid=103.
6. Stanislavski, *Legacy*, 20–21.
7. Ibid.

action and *feeling*, result *in natural life* on the stage in the form of one of the characters."[8] This is, of course, a simplification of what has been offered as Stanislavski's Method. However, looking specifically at these statements, the simplification is fair, and may remove the fear associated with the Method. Much of this fear and misunderstanding is related to the exercises that Stanislavski proposed in furtherance of the tenets of his System (e.g., sense memory and emotional memory are probably the most confusing to those who are not well read with regard to his work). One need only look at an illustration of his System (illustration P.1, page xiv) to feel overwhelmed.

In this book, specific attention will be given to these few tenets with exercises and embellishments provided by later practitioners. Discussions of items such as sense memory and emotional memory will occur, but should only be considered supplemental to the main points—items of interest that the reader can use or may ignore.

---

8. Stanislavski, *Legacy*, 21.

CHAPTER FIVE

Imagination and the Magical, Creative *If*

An understanding of the basic (and some advanced) concepts of acting, and experience with the practical application of those concepts, is paramount to a singer's ability to achieve a truthful and believable performance. First and foremost, believable acting is predicated on the singer's ability to imagine—to accept that the action of the opera, musical, or play is happening in real time to the performer. It is this concept that Stanislavski called the "magical, creative *if*" (or magic *if*), and it is the foundation of his System.[1]

> The actor says to himself: "All these properties, make-ups, costumes, the scenery, the publicness of the performance, are lies. I know I do not need any of them. But if they were true, then I would do this and this, and I would behave in this manner and this way towards this and this event.[2]

In other words, *if* I were truly in this situation, I would behave *this* way. Robert Blumenfeld further describes the magic *if* as follows:

> You behave *as if* the character had a past and *as if* the character has a future, unless, of course, the character dies in the course of the play. But before that happens, you continue to behave *as if* it were not going to. And you behave *as if* events have taken place when the character is not there, between the scenes of the play, and *as if* you have reacted to those events. You have to act *as if* the present time in which the character lives is your own (it is, actually). Most important of all, you have to behave *as if* every moment had never happened before and were occurring spontaneously.[3]

---

1. Constantin Stanislavsky, *My Life in Art*, trans. J.J. Robbins (Boston: Little, Brown and Company, 1924), 466.
2. Ibid.
3. Blumenfeld, *Stanislavski System*, 27.

Not only does the magic *if* free the actor or singer from creating an alter ego for each character he or she plays, it allows the actor or singer to work in the first person rather than the third. For example, a singer rehearsing the role of Mimì in Giacomo Puccini's *La bohème* can proceed from her own experiences, completing the statement "If I were in this situation, I would _____." It is the acceptance of a *given circumstance* as happening to the performer directly (as the character) that allows for the performer to become more intimately involved in the events. The required analysis of the character's actions becomes possible (as it would be impossible to look at a character from the outside and know what his or her motivations are).

The given circumstance is a crucial element of acting and the magic *if.* The given circumstance, loosely defined, is that situation in which the character finds him- or herself—that situation upon which the scene is predicated. In *An Actor Prepares*, Stanislavski explained the concept.

> *If* is the starting point, the given circumstances, the development. The one cannot exist without the other, if it is to possess a necessary stimulating quality. However, their functions differ somewhat: *if* gives the push to dormant imagination, whereas the *given circumstances* build the basis for *if* itself. And they both, together and separately, help to create an inner stimulus.[4]

The given circumstance is easily found but often overlooked or paid only cursory attention by the operatic performer. Yet without it, there is nothing in an opera to interest the audience. Juliet is a Capulet and Romeo a Montague, two families at war—this is a given circumstance. Mimì is dying of consumption[5]—this is a given circumstance. Charlotte is betrothed to Albert but in love with Werther—this is a given circumstance. These are the situations for which the performer can then ask the question "What *if?*"

Anyone who has rehearsed a conversation with a former lover or practiced quitting before meeting with his or her boss has used imagination as a tool of preparation. As children, imaginations create scenes rivaling that of our reality. When we play as children, the circumstances we create and the actions we undertake as a consequence of those circumstances can feel so real as to be difficult to release when required. This may be due to the fact that as children, the realities of our lives are somewhat protected and our

4. Constantin Stanislavski, *An Actor Prepares*, trans. and ed. Elizabeth Reynolds Hapgood (New York: Theatre Arts, 1961), 48.

5. Most singers familiar with *La traviata* or *La bohème* will recognize *consumption* as a word used during that period to refer to tuberculosis.

responsibilities do not rival or outweigh our need for recreation. Whatever the case, as adults, we tend to lose the vividness of imagination that we once had. Actors and singers alike must learn to re-energize imagination—to become more childlike in their belief of the alternate universe. Imagination exercises are typically simple to describe and to use, but require the actor or singer to do something much more difficult—one, concentrate, and two, believe.

An exercise for building (or reviving) one's imagination is as follows:

> Close your eyes and imagine someone that you are close to—someone that you love very dearly and someone whose loss would cause you emotional and physical pain. Concentrate on a specific context (e.g., you and this person are having dinner at your favorite restaurant and sitting at a small table across from one another). Paint this picture in your mind down to the smallest detail—what is he or she wearing, what color are his or her eyes and hair, what are the shapes of his or her ears, what are the two of you having for dinner and dessert, is it cold inside or outside, what sounds do you hear, and so forth. Concentrate on the lighting in the room and what it smells like (smell is a very important sense when it comes to memory). Be specific and do not ignore the small details. If the vision is detailed and you are able to concentrate on it, you should begin to feel, even if only for a second, that the image you have created is real and you are actually existing in that moment.

This exercise can and should be repeated daily. As most people are in their most relaxed and concentrative state as they lie in bed before falling asleep (generally speaking), this is an excellent time to do such work. The importance of relaxation and concentration will be discussed in the next chapter.

CHAPTER SIX

Relaxation and Concentration

S tanislavski believed that relaxation and concentration were not only essential for good acting work, they were its foundation. Physical tension is problematic for many reasons, the most important of which is that it often serves as a distraction. As singers, physical tension is especially concerning when it occurs in the singing mechanism. Singing teachers deal with back, abdominal, chest, shoulder, neck, and tongue tension as a matter of course. Fortunately, there is a mutually beneficial relationship between acting and singing in this regard (as well as others). Just as physical tension is the enemy of good singing, it is also the enemy of good acting.

RELAXATION

A singer's body is an instrument of interpretation. It must be free to move in the ways required to accurately interpret the libretto. If you (as your character) need to look at two people on opposite sides of the room, but you have problematic neck tension, the motion will be limited, if possible at all. It may seem silly, but it is important to understand. Many singers never consider how tension affects them as actors; they only consider the singing issues.

Relaxation, however, is simple to understand and to work on. It requires awareness only that there is tension, where it exists, and a conscious effort to release it through stretching. Persistent tension may need a systematic approach, but it can often be reduced or even alleviated. Severe tension will likely require a medical consultation.

During classes (or individually) in both singing and acting, an extraordinary amount of time should be devoted to stretching. The singers should be guided through relaxing various muscle groups with breathing techniques incorporated. An example of such an exercise is as follows:

1. The singer (or singers) lie on the floor in a position that

allows them to release their muscles without becoming uncomfortable. The singer begins to breathe in measured increments using a relaxed breath (one supported and suitable for singing sustained lines). For example, inhale for two counts and exhale for eight at the tempo of andante. As singers exhale, they should allow their muscles to become heavy, letting the floor hold them up (releasing participants of the responsibility of holding themselves up).

2. During the course of these breathing cycles, the singers should move their legs to one side, keeping their shoulders on the ground and turning their hips (releasing the lower back with each exhalation). This is repeated to the opposite side (first right, then left, or vice versa). Once the legs have returned to center, singers should roll into the "fetal position," resting for a moment and then continuing into the "child pose."[1] It is important to remember that the breathing cycle continues and all movements occur on the exhalation rather than the inhalation.

3. From the "child pose," the singers will breathe in for three and out for twelve while moving to their feet from the waist down. They will end in what is sometimes referred to as the "rag doll position." This position involves standing with slightly bent knees from the waist down, but bent at the waist with hands, arms, shoulders, neck, and head hanging. In this position, singers should not "hold" the neck, head, or shoulders, but rather let the weight of their heads pull them toward the floor. The "child pose" and the "rag doll position" are good opportunities to consider the back's function in breathing.

4. In the "rag doll position," singers should breathe in for two and out for eight. In six breathing "cycles," singers should "roll" up from the waist, concentrating on each vertebra—the shoulders, neck, and head are the last to roll up (respectively).

5. Once singers are in an upright position, they should drop their heads, keeping their shoulders back, and roll their heads from side to side, pausing when they feel tension. When singers

---

1. The "child pose" is simply a kneeling position in which the upper body is folded (the abdomen against the thighs and chest at the knees), the forehead set gently on the ground, and the arms stretched forward (or backward, depending on the instructor and the comfort of the participant). As many of these positions are inspired by yoga, more information on the positions can be found in several different books on the subject of yoga.

recognize a place of tension, they should breathe "into" the tension, exhaling to release it. Despite the placebo-like quality of this remedy, it often produces favorable results. Finally, the singers roll their heads into an upright position, shoulders back and down (opening the sternum to the audience), and the eyes focused up and out. For singers, it is crucial that they do not hold the muscles of the abdomen here, as this restricts breath support.

A further discussion of this exercise will occur in later chapters as a facilitation of emotional memory.

CONCENTRATION

Though many authors and scholars have devoted entire chapters to the two items, I find relaxation and concentration to be inextricably linked, especially with regard to singing. Though individual chapters could be devoted to them, I will follow the edict I set forth in this book to "boil down" the System. There are many books devoted to Stanislavski that will provide more information to those interested.

In the chapter of *An Actor Prepares* called "Concentration and Attention," the Director relays an elaborate and tragic tale of Maria and Kostya in order to illustrate a point about attention. Kostya is counting money for his job, and when finished, he joins Maria in another room to bathe their newborn son. Maria's younger brother, who has intently watched his brother-in-law work throwing the paper bindings into the fire, decides that he wants to see what color the fire will burn when fueled by papers in Kostya's work station. When Kostya returns, he pushes Maria's brother, Vanya, out of the way in an attempt to retrieve the final stack of papers. Seeing Vanya is injured, Maria attempts to revive him, only to find that he is bleeding. When she returns to the bath to get water, she discovers that her baby has drowned. Following the description of this scenario, the director asks a simple question: "Is this enough of a tragedy to keep your minds off the audience?"[2]

The fact that we as performers are unavoidably aware of being watched precludes us from being truthful. We become more concerned about what we look like as actors rather than how we tell the story. Think about the first time you went through a stack of performance photos and picked the ones that looked "right" or "interesting." Taken out of context, the most interesting photos are usually the ones based on some type of standardized gesture, pose,

---

2. Stanislavski, *Prepares*, 68–69.

or facial expression. Ask yourself if you act differently when you know there is a photographer in the audience or if you become more "intense" (than you are in the rehearsal room) when there is an audience in the dress rehearsal. Imagine for a moment that an old lover passes you in busy train station. Do you walk differently; in an attempt to look busy or important, do you look at your watch even though you had just done so moments before? There is little reality in performing differently when people are watching than you do in solitude. Concentration on stage is highly dependent on the singer's ability to *imagine*, and his or her belief in the given circumstance.

How is concentration on the stage possible with so many people watching? Stanislavski provides the following answer: "In order to get away from the auditorium you must be interested in something on the stage . . . an actor must have a point of attention and this point of attention must not be in the auditorium."[3]

Sanford Meisner, as we will see later, based much of his teaching on this tenet of the Method. As stated previously, Meisner believed that actors had two problems: they were self-conscience and they did not listen to each other—both are issues of concentration. After all, if actors believe what is happening on stage and are focused on that *reality*, they will lose awareness that they are being watched. Imagine having a thoroughly engrossing conversation with a friend in a crowded subway car. If you are focused on your friend and the conversation, you will not notice the man sitting across the aisle staring.

Earlier, I discussed the need to be physically relaxed in order to allow the body, as an instrument of performance, to facilitate the actions necessary to be truthful. This idea is not unlike that of the act of singing, as it requires physical relaxation for optimal efficiency. Just as physical relaxation is required for the body, mental relaxation is required for concentration. Mental relaxation requires releasing the concerns of the outside world. When the mind is clear, then and only then can the singer or actor focus on his or her partner in the scene.

To develop concentration on the objects on stage is to form a relationship with those items. A "sensory rehearsal" may seem a silly exercise, but is an effective way to begin to see properties (props) as belonging to you (as your character). Sensory rehearsals involve concentration on the character's personal belongings (e.g., a pen, hairbrush, locket, chair, and so forth—items important to the scene) while singing or reciting his or her lines. Holding the items—studying them for marks, texture, color, and weight—will make

---

3. Ibid., 70–71.

them familiar, and the singer will form a relationship with them. As with most exercises, a sensory rehearsal is a luxury often without the requisite time (especially in modern operatic rehearsal periods). However, property masters and stage managers, if asked nicely, may allow singers to use the actual props for rehearsal, given the props are available. At the very least, the actual props should be available to the singers during tech rehearsals, and simple investigation of these items will help to establish a relationship with them and improve concentration.

Concentration for singers is more difficult for at least one reason—there is a person beyond the edge of the stage who is waving his or her arms at the singer and expecting the singer to pay attention. The conductor cannot and should not be ignored, but the singer's attention must not be focused exclusively on the conductor. This is a delicate balancing act. During the rehearsal period, the singer must navigate where and when attention must be given exclusively to the conductor. This will allow for the most concentration possible to be devoted to the action on stage while giving due attention to the conductor. Most conductors (of the current generation) will only ask the singer to "check in" with them rather than stare. Asking for the location of the video monitors[4] at the beginning of staging rehearsals will help this process become more organic. For example, if the director would like the singer to look "down right" for a particular passage, if the singer knows that there is a monitor "house left,"[5] then he or she will feel more comfortable with this direction.

Despite the focus on concentration in his work, Stanislavski did not believe that concentration was absolute or that the performer should ignore the audience altogether. A theatrical performance is, after all, a give and take. Performers live their performances through the audience's reactions, and to ignore their input is antithetical to growth in a role. Stanislavski did, however, believe that the actor needed to concentrate on what was happening in the theatre and release his or her personal distractions from the outside. Stanislavski referred to this concentration, on the work and in front of an audience, as *public solitude*. For Stanislavski, the most important

---

4. A monitor often refers to a television screen projecting the images sent from a video camera trained on the conductor and placed over the audience (typically on the sides, but sometimes in the center). Monitors may also refer to audio speakers meant to project the sound of the orchestra onto the stage.

5. "Down right" refers to the part of the stage closest to the audience and to the singer's right (as he or she looks at the audience). By contrast, "house left" refers to the space beyond the proscenium (and the orchestra pit) and to the audience's left (as they look at the stage). "House left" and "down right" are actually on the same side of the theatre and based on the perspective of the observer (singer or audience).

element of public solitude was that of the *fourth wall*—the imaginary divider between audience and performer.

Lee Strasberg adopted this idea in the 1950s and developed an exercise he called the *private moment* (though most followers of Stanislavski would argue that these are two very different concepts). The private-moment exercise involves doing something private (but not personal or graphic) in front of a group of people. The private moment is something that one would do in life, but do only when alone and rarely if ever discuss. Clipping one's toenails or plucking one's eyebrows are examples of private moments. Strasberg would ask actors to do this exercise in front of their peers and found that they would be less inhibited afterward. However, Strasberg felt that the private-moment exercise only worked for those who had trouble communicating the reality of their feelings to an audience and did not recommend it for everyone.[6]

For Stanislavski, an actor onstage must focus on the character's necessary physical actions (and by default, his or her psychological justifications) with the same intensity required in his or her own life. For example, a letter read by a character onstage would require the same concentration as one read by the actor on the subway traveling to rehearsal.

Stanislavski divided concentration into what he referred to as "circles of attention." A small circle of attention may only be a few feet and include only a small number of items (e.g., a table, a chair, a candle, a pen and paper, and so forth). A small circle of attention may also include other characters, but is limited to a small group. For example, in act 1 of *Carmen*, Michaëla leaves Don José alone to read a letter from his mother. As he begins to read, his circle of attention is only himself, the chair he sits in, and the letter he is reading. This constitutes a small circle of attention.

A medium circle may include several people, props, and stage items such as furniture, but is smaller than the entire stage. A large circle of attention encompasses everything the actor can see on the stage (but not beyond). As the circle of attention grows to include more items and characters, it becomes more difficult to give full concentration to all things visible (not unlike in real life).[7]

Concentration requires observation. If one concentrates on an empty bottle on the table next to him or her, he or she will begin to notice things about the item that may have gone unnoticed previously (e.g., the color of the remaining liquid in the bottle, the font on the label, ingredients, etc.).

---

6. Robert H. Hethmon, ed., *Strasberg at the Actors Studio: Tape-Recorded Sessions* (New York: Theatre Communications Group, 1965), 116–117.
7. Sonia Moore, *The Stanislavski System* (New York: Penguin, 1977), 33–35.

Stanislavski believed that refocusing one's attention to a smaller circle could alleviate problems with large circles. If a singer is standing on a stage with a chorus, but focuses only on one person at a time, it will be less likely that his or her attention will begin to wane. A perfect example of this problem in opera exists in act 2, scene 2, of Carlisle Floyd's *Susannah*, in which Olin Blitch leads a revival and must stand in front of a large group (the chorus and other principals) telling them a particular story. If Olin Blitch attempts to relay the story to the whole group, he may not be able to hold his concentration level, but if he tells part of the story to one chorister or principal, then another, he will be less likely to lose his concentration and therefore tell a more effective story. This is true of any large chorus scene in opera.

Concentration (and the relaxation required to obtain it) allows for what is likely the most obvious and visible trait of good acting—*listening*. After all, one rarely listens when distracted (by people watching, tension in the body, and so forth). The next chapter will discuss listening and the problems associated with it.

CHAPTER SEVEN

The Importance of Listening

L ikely the most important skill under the larger heading of "Concentration" is the singer's ability to listen to those with whom he or she shares the stage. It seems that the most difficult item of the System, as well as the most important, is the ability to listen actively. Singers seem to find this task especially difficult, as it requires several supplementary skills. In order to listen actively and effectively on stage, one must first understand what Stanislavski and his progeny meant by listening, and how it resembles listening in life. The devotion of a chapter to listening, as opposed to its inclusion in "Concentration," is no accident. It is indicative of its importance and difficulty with regard to the singer.

In his book *The Actor's Ways and Means*, Michael Redgrave speaks of the art of listening on stage.

> For only a few actors "listen" all the time in the way that they should do, and every professional actor will be hurt if the director suggests to him that he is not really "listening." It is not only that some do not really "listen" at all but only hear, but there is the difference between listening in an artificial strained manner and listening as we listen in real life, which is to listen as spontaneously as we speak.[1]

The skill of listening seems to be especially difficult in opera, perhaps due to singers' proficiencies with foreign languages. However, the work that listening requires pales in comparison to the benefit it provides. Listening, and reacting honestly to what is being said, improves the singer's portrayal exponentially.

Whether directly or indirectly, the most significant work in listening was likely undertaken by Sanford Meisner. Meisner's work focused on the idea of remaining "in the moment," which required that actors react to what

---

1. Michael Redgrave, *The Actor's Ways and Means* (London: W. Heinemann, 1953), 60.

their partner in a scene was giving them. An exercise known simply as "Repetition" is crucial to Meisner's work in this area. Repetition will be discussed in detail later in this chapter.

WORKING MOMENT TO MOMENT

During a more than three-year tenure at the American Academy of Dramatic Arts, I was exposed to many new ideas that I found fascinating and enlightening. I had spent two years on the faculty of the Actors Studio Drama School (currently, the New School for Drama) and had found little to change my mind about Method actors. As most singers with little experience in acting technique, I thought Method actors were a cultlike group of obsessives. Whereas the Actors Studio Drama School had a direct line to Lee Strasberg's work at the Actors Studio and espoused a very strict application of Stanislavski's concepts (or a specific interpretation of those concepts), the American Academy of Dramatic Arts (AADA), the oldest acting conservatory in the English-speaking world, follows a Meisnerian approach. AADA is a fertile ground of creative thought, and the work that is undertaken there still holds influence over my understanding of theatre and acting. One of the aspects of the approach that I was immediately introduced to upon entering the doors of the Madison Avenue building was "moment to moment," or "working moment to moment."

At the midpoint of each term, the entire faculty would meet for three days to discuss common students and their issues in order to find a better and more cohesive approach to each student's problems. In all of my years of teaching and study, AADA is the only place in which the primary teacher (in this case, the acting teacher) had such a vested interest in a student's progress in peripheral skills. One of the first things that the acting teachers would discuss with the other instructors was the ability of a student to work moment to moment. It quickly became apparent to me how important this skill was for the student's success. Having had no training in this idea and not understanding what it meant, I took to observing acting classes at AADA in an attempt to understand and experience moment-to-moment work.

AADA, as mentioned in chapter 2, had undergone a few philosophical metamorphoses over the course of its existence. In the beginning, the techniques of Delsarte were taught, but they were eventually replaced by the techniques of Stanislavski. Currently, AADA teaches a Meisnerian approach. The idea of being "in the moment" or working moment to moment was not new as of Meisner, but AADA has focused on this ability and with it has had great success.

There is precious little written on Meisner and his work with actors. There is even less written by his own hand. Meisner's work was considered a great secret among the actors who studied with him. So little was written about his work, in fact, that Meisner's students produced a series of videos shortly before his death in order to record his approach. The tapes, now on DVD, are difficult to understand (and even more difficult to watch, especially for singers), as Meisner had repeated bouts with throat cancer and was only able to communicate by literally burping up words.

Like most great acting teachers of his generation, Sanford Meisner had been introduced to Stanislavski's Method and, in his own work, manipulated and modified it. Meisner first came into contact with Stanislavski's Method at the Group Theatre (where most American actors learned of Stanislavski) under the direction of Harold Clurman and Lee Strasberg. Meisner also worked with Stella Adler and Michael Chekhov, as well as Sudakov and Rappaport. In an interview published in 1964, Meisner discussed his interpretation of Stanislavski's System.

> The most important single element to me in Stanislavski, as also in Sudakov and Rappaport, is the reality of doing. An actor whose craft is securely rooted in the ability to live truthfully, which infers to do truthfully, under the imaginary circumstances of the play can perform in any style.[2]

Meisner's work was based on what he referred to as "the truth of acting" or "the ability to be real under imaginary circumstances." To Meisner, "Performances are not intellectual, but are impulsive."[3] In Meisner's work, there was also an element of urgency—*right now!* In discussing the "reality of doing" in his book *The Sanford Meisner Approach*, Larry Silverberg makes the following observation:

> There is a great mistake, something is very wrong in the theatre today. The majority of our theatre is a theatre where nothing is really happening, nothing is really happening *right now*. Not only is *right now* all that we have available to us in life, it is absolutely the key to *LIFE* on the stage. Yet most actors are reproducing what has been done before. Attempting to repeat what "clicked" in rehearsal or to recapture what "wowed!" last night's audience.[4]

---

2. Vera Soloviova, Stella Adler, Sanford Meisner, and Paul Gray, "The Reality of Doing," *The Tulane Drama Review* 9, vol. 1 (Autumn 1964): 155, 136–155.
3. Mark Bailey, *Notes on the Meisnerian Method*, Stella Adler and Harold Clurman Papers, Harry Ransom Center, University of Texas at Austin.
4. Larry Silverberg, *The Sanford Meisner Approach: An Actor's Workbook* (New Hampshire: Smith and Kraus,1994), 2.

The ability to be impulsive, truthful, and fresh in every moment of a play despite the weeks of rehearsal—as if the actor does not know (as the character) what will come next or what will happen to him or her—is working moment to moment. Stanislavski's discovery of the System is actually based on this idea. After all, as mentioned previously, it was Stanislavski's feeling that a role had become stale that caused him to embark on developing the System. Sadly, this is a concept rarely if ever discussed with singers. The prevailing thought seems to be that the addition of a predetermined rhythm and tempo precludes the singer from working in this way. Or simply, those who teach acting to singers are unaware of the significance of being in the moment.

The importance of moment-to-moment work can be seen in the growth a theatrical production experiences (the difference between the first run-through and the last) and the utter consistency seen on the operatic stage. Actors are encouraged (with some exceptions) to allow their impulses to take them in new directions, whereas consistency is prized in operatic productions. This focus on "sameness" stunts the growth of a production. At the very least, in educational settings such as acting classes and university or conservatory productions, singers should be allowed to experiment with moment-to-moment work. After all, "foolish consistency is the hobgoblin of little minds."[5] Uta Hagen articulated moment-to-moment work this way:

> We rehearse . . . in order to unearth and eventually to select the behavior that will most pertinently reveal each moment of the life of a particular human being caught up in the events prescribed by a playwright . . . Once that has been accomplished, the actor faces one of his most difficult technical problems: how to repeat the selected actions at every performance moment to moment, as if for the first time . . . It is achieved by a suspension of knowledge of what is to come, by "forgetting" everything except what is needed at the moment.[6]

With regard to later discussions of objectives, obstacles, and actions, it stands to reason that a character would have no precognitive knowledge that an action taken in furtherance of an objective would succeed in overcoming or fail to overcome the obstacle. This is especially true when working against the wants and needs of other characters in the scene. Though you, as the

---

5. Ralph Waldo Emerson, "Self-Reliance," *Essays, First and Second Series* (Boston: Houghton Mifflin, 1883), 58.
6. Uta Hagen, *A Challenge for the Actor* (New York: Maxwell Macmillan International, 1991), 164.

performer, know that Nemorino will take the contract from you at the beginning of "Prendi," Adina may expect Nemorino to throw the contract back at her (sophisticated musicians may also notice the rather "careful" music Donizetti provides Adina for this moment and assume she may be trying not to scare him away or upset him). "We never know whether we will succeed or fail in fulfilling our wishes until *after* the fact."[7]

Many acting teachers share a similar story that illustrates the concept of moment to moment. It involves a performance in which actors are onstage performing lines in a play. As the actors perform a particularly dramatic scene, a cat (at least in one version of the story) wanders onto the stage and begins to bathe himself. As if there were nothing else happening, the audience is immediately and uncontrollably drawn to the cat, from which they cannot turn. The acting teacher's point: *being* is much more interesting than *acting*. Research and character analysis are monumentally important, but they cannot be evident to the audience. This presents a conundrum: the singer must prepare for the scenes but not look as if the scenes have been prepared. Blumenfeld writes,

> Knowing but then forgetting is the actor's job in every event. However, in pre-Freudian plays of earlier times, it certainly helps actors to understand fully what psychological forces may be driving their characters, but in the end they must remain innocent of them in order to play the character.[8]

The idea of remaining innocent of future events is encapsulated in the concept of existing in a character's given circumstance, discovering each new emotion as it happens and as if it has not happened before (either at all or in the same fashion), listening or observing, and reacting truthfully. This is being in the moment or working from moment to moment. In common, nontheatrical vernacular, the idea of being in the moment is the same as it is in the theatre—to ignore the past and the future and focus on the present.

Blumenfeld's definition of moment to moment is "playing a scene without anticipating the next event in it, and allowing it to unfold naturally and organically in the time it takes for each beat."[9] This is likely the most challenging of all acting concepts to understand and to put into practice. The challenge for singers is compounded by the fact that rhythm, tempo, and the musical arc are largely (if not completely) controlled by

---

7. Ibid., 165.
8. Robert Blumenfeld, *Tools and Techniques for Character Interpretation; A Handbook of Psychology for Actors, Writers, and Directors* (New York: Limelight, 2006), xii.
9. Blumenfeld, *Dictionary*, 171.

the composer's score and the conductor's interpretation. The most notable exceptions to this rule are that of spoken dialogue found in *opéra comique*, *Singspiel*, operetta, musical theatre, and secco recitative. Nevertheless, the closer a singer can get to total immersion in the moment, the better his or her acting performance will be.

Perhaps the most important skills for the singer to acquire in order to remain in the moment are those of listening (as if what is being said has never been said before), observing (as if what is happening has never happened before), and reacting in real time (as if the singer is not aware of what is to come). For this, an exercise employed by Sanford Meisner in his teaching known as "Repetition" may be useful.

MEISNER'S REPETITION

The purpose of Meisner's Repetition exercise is to bring the focus of the actor to his or her partner and to simply "be present" in that moment (not concerned with outside distractions such as "There are people watching me" or "I would really like a steak for dinner"). The exercise is meant to bring actors to the point of simply listening, observing, and reacting to each other without the concerns of the activity's outward appearance— much like having an intense conversation with a friend on a noisy bus or subway car (which requires concentration and public solitude). Herein lies the single most important idea behind truthful acting or *representational* acting as a whole—to listen, observe, and react honestly (from the actor's own experience).

For the singer, Repetition can be an invaluable tool, but it also requires much more effort, especially when working in languages in which the singer is not fluent. Reacting not only to the meaning of the text, but also to the structure and nuance of the text, requires that singers be at least familiar with the structure of the language of the opera. It also requires that they translate not only their roles but the entire show, and know, word for word and contextually, what is being said to them. As most young singers (and some professionals) are reluctant to translate word for word their own texts, this demands a change in the approach to the work, as well as preparation for staging rehearsals. For study purposes, however, Repetition can and should be done in the singer's native language.

The Repetition exercise begins with two actors (or singers) sitting in chairs facing each other. The first observation, made by one actor of the other, can be based on appearance ("You are wearing a red shirt"), expression or posture ("You are smiling"), or emotion ("You are sad"). The second party responds by repeating the observation and changing the pronoun ("I am smiling"). The objective is to listen and react, focusing only on the interaction between actor and partner. This singular focus on the present circumstances, as discussed earlier, is working in the moment, or moment to moment. It removes the outer distractions of audience or class from the given task. The idea of being present in the moment and staying connected with a scene partner or partners is encapsulated in the popular adage "Acting is reacting." In other words, successful actors or singers need simply listen to (and observe) their partners and react honestly in order to present themselves truthfully on stage.

The Repetition exercise continues as the partners repeat the observations until something changes, which leads to a different observation. For example, if actor 1 observes that his partner is smiling, and as a result starts to laugh, the reaction of actor 2 ("I am smiling") changes to an observation ("You are laughing"). A true circumstantial connection to one's partner begins to unfold with the simple acts of listening, observing, and reacting.

An advanced element of Repetition—and ultimately, truthful acting—is represented in what Meisner referred to as the "Three Moment Game."[10] Listening and reacting honestly also involves observation that can lead to a deeper interpretation of the partner's motives or feelings about what is being said. When a person asks a loved one if he or she wants a soft drink and the loved one says, "Yes," while beginning to cry, the conversation will logically move in a new direction (due to the unexpected reaction). If someone asks a friend how she is feeling and she responds, "I'm fine," while looking sadly at the floor, the conversation will immediately turn toward the truth of the moment rather than where it would have gone if the physical reaction had mirrored the verbal response. The first moment is the verbalized observation ("You look happy"), the second is the physical reaction of the partner (crying), and the third is the verbalization of an observation based on the physical reaction ("You are crying" or "You are sad," and so forth). Meisner called this the Three Moment Game, but the number of moments is infinite. The point of this form of Repetition was to add observation of physical behavior (and emotional context) to listening and reacting.

Repetition exercises are not limited to the act of listening and reacting in a vacuum. Instead, they graduate in difficulty by adding items such as repetition with activities (an actor or both actors are given tasks such as knitting or writing letters around which they do the Repetition exercise). If one participant is given the task of solving a Rubik's Cube during Repetition,

---

10. Meisner, Barter, and Pollack, *Meisner Master Class* DVD.

the act of solving the cube becomes a circumstance that informs the observation and reaction. Actor 1 may say, "You seem to be having trouble solving your puzzle." This statement is repeated by actor 2 (with pronouns replaced). However, if actor 2 solves a side of the puzzle and shows pleasure at this, actor 1 may be compelled to react by saying, "You seem pleased."

A third version of the exercise adds a situational element, taking the exercise into the realm of complete improvisation. For example, actor 1 exits the room and then reenters, beginning the exercise. Actor 2 is compelled to react to actor 1's entrance, or perhaps the way that actor 1 enters the room. For example, if actor 1 enters and accidentally slams the door, the repetition may begin with "You slammed the door." However, if actor 1 reacts sheepishly in his or her repetition, it may lead actor 2 to observe that actor 1 is embarrassed, leading to "You are embarrassed" or "You don't seem angry." If we consider the edict that actors should listen and react truthfully within the given circumstances, then the addition of situational elements to the Repetition exercise represents the addition of the given circumstances to *listening* and *reacting truthfully*.

Though used primarily as a training tool in the classroom, some Meisner practitioners use Repetition as a means to garner focus before or even during rehearsals. Unlike the theatre, however, opera productions are afforded much less staging time and typically share rehearsals with musical concerns. For the training of singers, Repetition is likely a tool best used in the classroom, in scene rehearsals, or in scholastic productions. However, using this tool will help lay the groundwork for a more successful professional stage performance in the long run.

It is necessary for singers to be intimately familiar with the concepts of the *magic if, objective, obstacle, action, working moment to moment,* and *listening, observing,* and *reacting*. These concepts are most easily learned as part of formal acting classes. It would be difficult for these concepts to be absorbed simply through reading about them. Acting classes allow for experimentation and the practical application of these concepts to scripts (or libretti) in a less pressurized environment than that of a professional rehearsal. Acting classes also provide the student with something often lacking in professional rehearsals—feedback. Singers should not fear entering an acting class based simply on inexperience. Everyone has to start somewhere.

PART III

ACTION AND FEELING: THEATRICAL SYNERGY

CHAPTER EIGHT

Action

Merriam-Webster defines the term *act* (or *to act*) as "to represent or perform by action esp. [*sic*] on the stage."[1] The presence of the word *action* in this definition may not seem noteworthy; however, the concept of action is crucial in the understanding of Stanislavski's work.

PHYSICAL ACTION

In her book *Stanislavski and the Actor*, Jean Benedetti breaks action down into two main categories: physical action and mental action. Benedetti illuminates the importance of physical action this way: "Physical action is the basis of acting. This is what an audience sees, interprets—movement, stance, gesture—to understand the meaning of the play."[2] If a character has nothing but inner life, blank stares, withheld emotional reactions, and so forth, there is nothing for an audience to witness—and ultimately, nothing for them to relate to. If a character does not cry or put her head in her hands or laugh, how would the audience know of her inner emotional state? It is the conversion of the inner emotional life into physical action that is at the epicenter of all acting methods. Physical action is also necessary in the movement of the play or opera itself. If Canio does not stab Nedda at the end of *Pagliacci*, the opera has no resolution. If Nemorino never drinks the elixir, the subsequent events in *L'elisir d'amore* would be different, leading to a different conclusion. It was physical action that was the end result of the System, thus the name *The Method of Physical Action*, which Blumenfeld defines as "the essential Stanislavsky system. Its basic premise is that every action taken by a character has a psychological motivation."[3] All other tenets of the System or Method roll downhill toward what the audience will actually experience and interpret—physical action.

---

1. Merriam-Webster's Collegiate Dictionary, 11th ed., s.v. "opera."
2. Jean Benedetti, *Stanislavski and the Actor* (New York: Routledge, 1998), 16.
3. Blumenfeld, *Dictionary*, 166.

The beginning of this process of physical action involves awareness of the actor's muscles (identifying and releasing tension, examining natural actions, and so forth) and ends with justification through intent. It is the justification of physical action that seems to elude young singers. Young singers with little training in acting need often be told that they should not move (especially their feet) unless they have a reason to do so. I once worked with a young soprano who paced almost uncontrollably. In addition to explaining to her that she should move only "for a specific purpose," I was, at times, forced to get on my knees and hold her feet to the floor so that she would remain in the same place. It is important to note at this point that standing still is not the same as "park and bark." Humans do stand still at times.

MENTAL ACTION

Whereas physical action is the recognizable element of acting, mental action occurs as the precursor to physical action. Mental action consists of the stimuli that create physical action—focus and concentration, imagination, subtext, and emotional memory. If action were a chicken, these items would constitute the egg (assuming one believes that the egg came first). Mental action is the starting point.

Clarity of this idea will come in the chapter on objectives, obstacles, and actions. The objectives and obstacles help to create the mental actions required for the physical action. For example, if the character is hungry (and the actor feels that hunger through imagination or sense memory), then an objective is formed ("I want to eat") followed by an obstacle ("I have no food") and finally a physical action ("I drive to a restaurant").

For Stella Adler, actions were regarded as strong or weak largely based on the specificity with which the actor chose the action.[4] A strong action, for example, should be doable and should have a clear starting and ending point. Action should not be confused with its justification. For example, "I am thirsty" is the why, but not the how. The action attached to such a motivation is "I drink water." This action also represents a strong action because it is specific, whereas "I drink something" is not specific and would be categorized as weak. Adler also broke down actions into what, where, when, and why. What, where, and when are part of the given circumstances—for example, "I have a beer at McGinty's Pub on Third Avenue in New York City at 10 pm on Friday, June 3, 1964." The addition of "why" creates a more interesting and still strong choice ("I need to kill time while waiting

---

4. Stella Adler, *The Technique of Acting* (New York: Bantam, 1990), 35–36.

for a friend who is late"). Large actions must be broken into smaller actions. It is important to understand that acting is based on physical action, but physical action requires mental action. In the next few chapters, a formula will begin to emerge (objective + obstacle = action). This formula should be part of every scene study.

Often with young singers, actions can be well prepared but poorly executed. This is most often due to a lack of clarity. The director has given the singer a bit of blocking, and the singer executes the action considering the "why" and making the action or "stage business" his or her own—and by result, the character's. The most important aspect of physical action is specificity. Physical choices that are unclear in the mind of the singer or actor will be unclear to the audience. Psychological justification of those actions, if not well prepared by the singer or actor, will also produce an action that is weak or vague. The audience's only clues to the character are in the character's words and actions, so specificity is crucial. Librettists make specific choices in building characters; composers choose specific chords, intervals, and even silences to create an atmosphere for each character. Singers must also be specific.

CHAPTER NINE

Affective Memory

Tommaso Salvini, one of Verdi's favorite stage actors, said, "The great actor should be full of feeling, and especially he should feel the thing he is portraying. He must feel an emotion not only once or twice while he plays it, no matter whether it is the first or the thousandth time."[1] In other words, an actor must have the ability to ask the question "How would I feel *if?*," feel the feelings associated, and portray these feelings over and over again. Herein lies one of the conundrums facing singers: How can I feel something so deeply (that may bring me to physical pain or tears) and still sing beautifully?

A singer once told me a story: During a performance of a new opera based on a famous play, she "forgot" herself onstage and began to think about the pain her character must be feeling in that moment. The thought brought about an intense feeling of loss, and she began to lose control of her emotions, almost coming to tears on stage. The singer, a young soprano, explained that after the performance, a friend approached her and told her how moving that scene was to him—more wonderful than he had ever seen her. She exclaimed that it was "horrible" and that she had barely held it together in order to get through the scene. My response: "No one said being good was easy." Her story amazed and perplexed me. Here was a young soprano who had moved her audience by experiencing those emotions appropriate to the scene through her imagination. Yet she felt the experience to be an undesirable occurrence.

I preface this chapter with this story because it seems that most singers are afraid of being vulnerable emotionally on stage due to the physical vulnerability that occurs. After all, vocal technique is often fragile, and involuntary movement of the diaphragm or closing of the throat (things that occur when a person becomes "choked up") are incredibly problematic when one is also expected to produce beautiful sounds. Often, because of

1. Stanislavski, *Prepares*, 13.

this, acting takes a back seat to singing. Much of this fear comes from the fact that voice teachers (generally speaking) do not attempt to help singers interpret (physically) what they are singing and rarely ask for more than a good, technically produced singing sound. The most important person in a singer's training rarely if ever asks him or her to sing with an emotional context, resulting in an inability to do so when necessary. When singers reach the stage, and they are required to describe what they are singing and how they (as the characters) feel, many become self-conscious and even defensive.

Emotional context is paramount to the work of an actor and a singer. Consider the earlier chapter on the *magic if.* You ask yourself not only what you would *do* if, but also how you would *feel* if. There is an element of the chicken and the egg here, but mostly you *do* something because you *feel* something. The feeling is literally the vanguard of the action.

How do we access these feelings—not only once but over and over again and freshly each time? After all, a singer or actor must first work in the conscious before finding the subconscious.[2] This discussion involves some rather complex and often confusing terms. Different practitioners of the System call them different things, all based in Stanislavski's own words. The terms are *affective memory, sense memory, emotional recall,* and *emotion memory* or *emotional memory.* Before illuminating the differences, it is beneficial to understand from where these terms originated.

The term *affective memory* was first coined by French psychologist Théodule-Armand Ribot (not to be confused with the painter, Théodule-Augustin Ribot) and came to the attention of Stanislavski through Ribot's book *La Psychologie des Sentiments.*[3] It is difficult to construct a clear definition for *affective memory* through this and earlier writings by Ribot. However in 1895, shortly after Ribot's first publications on the subject, E. B. Titchener published the following definition:

> By "affective memory" we can, of course, mean two different things. We may mean the power of voluntarily recalling a past affection. In this sense, memory implies the working of attention. In order to voluntarily recall an experience, we focus the attention upon all its constituent processes, until the experience itself is reproduced, in apparent completeness, in obedience to the laws of association or apperceptive combination. But we may also mean to express by the term "memory" the fact that affection is revivable: that a past pleasure-pain may appear in consciousness in virtue of its revivability, just as a past perception may appear in idea, as representation.

2. Stanislavski, *Prepares,* 14.
3. Pitches, 91.

Here the active attention need not be involved; the affection may be supposed to arise "of itself," the consequence of the automatic working of the laws of mental association.[4]

As will be seen later in this chapter, it is the former with which the actors of the Stanislavski school are concerned. Again, it is important to note that Stanislavski abandoned his work on affective memory later in his life, but many of his followers (Strasberg chief among them) refused.

As for the reality of affective memory, Ribot himself acknowledged dissent among his peers regarding its viability and even found that only some people had the capacity for it. Whether or not its validity can be challenged, affective memory's place in Stanislavski's early work is undeniable. It is the most controversial tenet of the Method and for some, the most important. Though Stanislavski eventually abandoned this work, it is included in this book so that an understanding may be reached. Affective memory is still taught in certain circles, and a young singer or actor is likely to hear the term in his or her acting studies.

An explanation of what affective memory is with regard to acting may be best left to Richard Boleslavsky (credited as the first to bring Stanislavski's work to America and codify principles of the System in his own book, *Acting: The First Six Lessons*, initially published several years before *An Actor Prepares*). *Acting: The First Six Lessons* is written as a dialogue between Boleslavsky ("I") and a young student (the "Creature"). During this discussion of affective memory, Boleslavsky explains to the "Creature" that all artists possess a specific capacity to remember not just situations but the feelings associated with the emotions tied to those situations. These memories can be evoked by the senses (such as smell and taste). To illuminate his point, Boleslavsky tells the story of a couple who have been married for two decades. The two become engaged during a stroll in a cucumber patch. During the stroll, the two would smell the cucumbers and even eat them. Cucumbers were even served at their wedding. After several difficult years of marriage, no matter how much they argued, the couple's mood would always lighten when for dinner they would eat fresh cucumbers. The cucumbers reminded them of a happier time in their lives and would, in turn, make them happy. Afterward, Boleslavsky asked the young actor if she understood the concept:

THE CREATURE: [*very brightly*] Yes, the outward circumstances brought back the inward feelings.

---

4. E. B. Titchener, "Affective Memory," *The Philosophical Review* 4, no. 1 (Jan. 1895): 65–76.

I: I wouldn't say feelings. I would say rather, made these two people what they were long years before, in spite of time, reason, and maybe—desire, *unconsciously*.[5]

Boleslavsky's point, as he continues in the book, is that actors have a fountain of memories that are so strong they can be recalled, once awakened. These feelings can be controlled and finally used on stage.[6] The use of such feelings or memories is called *substitution*. Blumenfeld defines substitution as

> the actor's conscious replacement of the fictitious objects, emotions, events, people, relationships, or places with objects from the actor's private life. Substitution is one of the most important tools used to bring reality to the character portrayal. In performance, the actor must relate directly to the other actor: substitution is therefore a rehearsal (rather than a performance) tool, and should be forgotten by the time the actor gets to the performance stage.[7]

Edward Dwight Easty provides perhaps the most concise definition of affective memory in his book *On Method Acting*.

> Affective Memory is the conscious creation of remembered emotions which have occurred in the actor's *own* past life and then their application to the character being portrayed on stage . . . In order to make a character come *alive* on stage, the emotions, thoughts, and feelings of the character must be real to the actor. He must learn to search his own past for emotions that will correspond to his character's life.[8]

A young singer once asked me to coach her on "Una voce poco fa," from Rossini's *Il barbiere di Siviglia*. This particularly talented mezzo was twenty-eight years old and had been married for a few years. As I watched her, it dawned on me that she was singing this role from her perspective. I asked her how old she thought Rosina was. She replied, "A teenager."

"As a teenager and given her current circumstances, she has probably never felt love before meeting Lindoro (Almaviva). Correct?"

"Probably not."

I then asked her to attempt to remember what it was like to have her first real crush—the intensity of the feelings, the pulse of awakening hormones,

---

5. Robert Boleslavsky, *Acting: The First Six Lessons* (New York: Theatre Arts Books, 1956), 36–38.
6. Ibid., 38–39.
7. Blumenfeld, *Dictionary*, 276.
8. Edward Dwight Easty, *On Method Acting* (New York: Ballantine, 1992), 44–45.

and the rather ridiculous idea (that everyone experiences around that age) that first love will last forever. I wanted her to sing the aria from *that* perspective (not the twenty-eight and married perspective). The mezzo was intrigued. She understood the logic and the benefit of that interpretation, but had no idea how to accomplish this, given that she was *not* in that situation. In a case such as this, an affective memory exercise might be useful.

I was fortunate enough to study Shakespearean acting in graduate school, though I was not studying to be an actor but rather a director. The class was, to say the least, a challenge, but one of the most beneficial in all of my training. During one class period, a student was working on a monologue from *Romeo and Juliet*. She was having trouble accessing the appropriate emotions for the character (in this case, jubilation) and was working rather mechanically. After several minutes, the teacher stopped her and said, "I want you to close your eyes and imagine your proudest moment. What is it?"

"When I won the high school state championship in tennis," said the girl.

"Fine. Close your eyes and try to imagine the moment when you hit the winning point. Focus so vividly on the moment that you can hear the crowd and smell the air."

The girl, standing center stage with her eyes closed and in front of all of her colleagues, began to smile. The more she focused on the moment four years prior, the more she felt the feelings associated with it. At the moment that she seemed to reach the most vivid memory of the feeling, the teacher said, "Now, be Juliet in that moment." The change in the performance was immediate and unmistakable. The teacher had directed the student to access her emotional memory in order to find her way into the scene.

SENSE MEMORY

There has been, at times, confusion as to the sameness of emotional memory and sense memory. Emotional memory, affective memory, and the "memory of feelings" (as it has also been translated) are, in fact, the same.[9] The terms *sense memory* and *affective* or *emotional memory* are often used interchangeably, though this is incorrect. As the senses can be tied to emotions, they are closely related, however technically different, entities. Uta Hagen describes the difference between and relation of the two as follows:

> I link "emotional memory" with the recall of a *psychological* or emotional response to an event moving in on me which produces sobbing, laughter, screaming, etc. I use the term "sense memory" in dealing with *physiological*

9. Easty, 44.

sensations (heat, cold, hunger, pains, etc.). Of course, it is true that a physical sensation such as heat or cold can produce emotions such as irritation, depression or anxiety; likewise, an emotional response can be accompanied by or produce physical sensations (such as getting hot or goose-pimply, becoming nauseated).[10]

To add to the confusion, the two have also been referred to (collectively) as *affective memory*. Robert Blumenfeld defines affective memory as "the memory of emotions and feelings, called *emotional memory*, and the memory of physical sensations, called *sense memory*. Emotional and sense memories overlap: every sense memory involves an emotional memory; every emotional memory involves the senses."[11]

For Stanislavski, there was a distinct difference between sense memory (or *sensation memory* as he called it in *An Actor Prepares*) and emotional memory or affective memory, though he did feel that they ran "parallel to one another."[12] Sense memory was even thought to be an element of emotional memory or "for the purpose of influencing our emotion memory."[13] So what is it?

Simply put, sense memory is remembering with the five senses—or as Uta Hagen defined it, "the recall of physical sensations."[14] Everyone who has had to describe a suspicious pain to a doctor or a bitterly cold evening to a friend has experienced sense memory. When I was about ten years old, I fell off my bike traveling down a friend's steep and rocky driveway. The front wheel locked, casting me headlong off of the bike. As I braced for the impact, I put my hands out, hitting my left palm on the rocky ground first. The impact tore my skin at the palm, and I remember distinctly feeling a surge of pain, but more interestingly, heat on my palm. Often when remembering lovers, people will discuss the scent of their perfume or the feel of their skin. All are examples of sense memory.

The relationship of the two memories can be seen in the last example. A memory of how someone's skin feels or the smell of her perfume or his cologne will almost always produce at least a small emotional reaction. One can evoke an emotional memory by first setting the scene with the senses. For example, it has been stated that smell is the sense most closely tied to memory. We smell something that reminds us of a time or setting and we remember the feeling. Immediately after graduation from high school, I

10. Hagen, *Respect*, 46–47.
11. Blumenfeld, *Dictionary*, 9.
12. Stanislavski, *Prepares*, 159.
13. Ibid., 184.
14. Hagen, *Respect*, 52.

began touring the country with a musical organization. We rode on buses, and our equipment was carried in large trucks. During the course of our performances, the buses and trucks would idle in the parking lot, so there was an overwhelming scent of diesel fuel when we arrived at the buses after a performance. To this day, that odor evokes an intense feeling of nostalgia, and I am immediately transported to that time twenty years ago. This is an example of sense memory.

In the classes that I have taught, I have often employed a physical warmup that involves stretching, breathing, and relaxation set to music that I selected prior to the class. During the evolution of this exercise, I began to ask my singers to "tune in" to the music that they were hearing. As stated in an earlier chapter, the progression of this warmup begins typically on the floor and then, using a series of breathing exercises timed to movement, progresses through different positions, finally ending in a standing position. At the end of this exercise, I began asking students to keep their eyes closed and listen to the music that was being played (often, this music was a lament to a lost lover or of a melancholy mood, though not always). I would then ask the students to think of someone close to them—perhaps a lover, family member, or friend. I asked the singers to imagine said individual not just visually, but with all five of their senses: What does he or she look like? What is he or she wearing, and if you could touch his or her hand, what would the skin feel like? And, lastly, what does he or she smell like (e.g., what cologne or perfume reminds the singer of that person)? I simply guide the students to remember with every means available.

I eventually began to ask the students to imagine that the person they had been concentrating on was suddenly to die or vanish, never to be seen again. Many of the singers would well up with tears—the emotional imagination so strong that real and true feelings came to the surface. Turning that outward to the work at hand, one can see how effective a tool sense memory and, by its association, emotional memory can be. Music is especially important in these exercises, as much of our lives are now lived with a soundtrack (iPods in our ears constantly), not unlike opera.[15]

How do we access these memories? There are many acting exercises that

---

15. Singers often ask why it is necessary in acting exercises to focus the imagination on negative experiences such as death or romantic loss. They often feel that they spend too much of their time in acting classes crying. I explain to them, though I have no scientific or psychological evidence to support it, that sadness is the easiest emotion to access, because it is held just below the surface. Many times, people who have just gone through a trauma or loss of some sort will respond, "I'm good," to the question "How are you today?" I have found that all one needs to release the true emotion is an assurance that it is okay to do so, and many imagination exercises provide that.

deal with sense memory and emotional memory. However, the imagination of the singer is the catalyst for all memories, including those needed for the theatre. A singer need only attempt to remember, in detail, a former lover, a good meal, a significant moment in his or her life, and so forth, by concentrating on it and recreating it in the imagination, focusing on specific details. Accessing the memories is never difficult—most creative people are highly imaginative. The problem is finding the correct memory for the situation and applying it to the work at hand.

How are these memories useful? This is answered in the definitions of *substitution* and *endowment*. In order for memories to be helpful to a singer, the singer must be able to endow the imaginary circumstances with his or her personal and recalled emotions (emotions belonging to a memory in the singer's own life). See page 72 for Blumenfeld's definition of substitution.

Endowment is described by Blumenfeld as "the projection of physical or emotional qualities onto an object or person in order for the actor endowing the object or person to relate in a personal, real way." In this definition, Blumenfeld also sums up the System: "All acting is endowment: to treat the given circumstances as real is to endow fictitious life with reality."

Of all of Stanislavski's principles, affective memory is likely the most difficult for singers, as it requires physical, mental, and emotional release. The accessing of sense memories or emotional memories is not difficult. Humans do this on a daily basis. Though affective memory became less and less important in Stanislavski's teachings later in life, many acting teachers still use it as a tool for building a point of view within the actor. Affective memory is an interesting tool for experimentation in class and rehearsal, but can also be risky for a singer whose vocal technique requires relaxation (as all good techniques do) as well as command of all of the muscles.

I have used emotional exercises in my work with singers (mostly university and conservatory students) to high degrees of success. The following is an exercise (described earlier) that I have used to create a fertile emotional environment prior to acting work or to operatic staging rehearsals.

Adding Emotional Recall to Relaxation

Music should be played softly in the background but with enough volume to enter the mind of the singers participating in the exercise. As music is a crucial element of their stage lives, so too is it important in acting exercises for singers. The type of music played is critical. The exercise leader must plan what particular emotion they wish the singer to recall and pick music based on that idea. After all, Mimì does not die to the joyful Christmas sounds of act 2. The following exercise incorporates the relaxation work from chapter 5. The exercise leader will introduce a narrative while the participants follow the sequence. The narrative will require a specific situation with enough flexibility to be applicable to the individual participants (e.g., "Imagine someone you have lost—either a breakup, a friend who no longer speaks to you, or a death . . . "). During the course of the sequence, the narrative will become more specific and, for maximum effect, timed to points of interest in the music. Think of this exercise as a movie soundtrack or an operatic score.

1. Lie down on the floor with your feet flat and knees up (so that your back can expand against the floor as you breathe).

2. Breathe in measured increments (e.g., in for two counts, out for eight). This is a particularly good time for the singer to check in with his or her breathing technique and to relax the muscles of the body.

3. During the different breathing sequences, move your knees to the left or right, keeping your shoulders on the ground in order to stretch the lower back. During this process, the expansion of the back becomes more evident to the singer as the muscles tighten and release.

4. After proper stretching of the lower back, use one full breathing sequence to roll into the fetal position either to the left or to the right (the side doesn't matter). Follow this with a breathing sequence that allows you to roll into the "child pose" (see the description in chapter 6).

5. During a longer breathing sequence (e.g., inhale for three and exhale for twelve), get onto your feet, remaining bent at the waist—head, arms, and shoulders released and hanging toward the floor (the "rag doll position").

6. During a cycle of breathing sequences (six repeated sequences of in for two and out for eight), roll up one vertebra at a time until you are in a standing, upright position. Your head should be the last part to reach the upright position.

7. Using the music playing in the background, think about the emotion you feel for the person you have loved most in your life whether it be a relative, a friend, or a lover. Focus specifically on that feeling. Imagine the way he or

she smells, what he or she looks like in his or her clothing, the color of his or her hair, the feel of his or her skin when you touch it, and so forth. Imagine the physical sensation that occurs when you see him or her or hear his or her voice. Spend a few minutes building a very detailed mental picture of this person. It may take a few attempts to build physical sensations in this imaginary circumstance. Keep trying.

8. With your eyes still closed, imagine that person is suddenly removed from your life. If you have lost this person in reality, remember the feeling of losing him or her. Put yourself in a place where that person no longer exists. Allow yourself to feel that loss.

This exercise may be attempted with other emotions. Whatever the emotion, it must be tangible and strong. Appropriate music will help the participants to access these feelings. It is also crucial to allow recovery time after this exercise.

CHAPTER TEN

Units, Bits, and Beats

O f all of the elements of acting technique used in the training of singers and in the staging of operas, the word *beat* (the acting term, not the musical term) is likely the most prevalent. Directors will use this word (e.g., "There is a *beat* here,") and singers will nod their heads in agreement, despite the fact that most are unaware of its actual meaning. Most singers have a general idea of what is meant by beat, but the fact is that Stanislavski's use of this concept has become somewhat obscured. The word *beat* grew to replace Stanislavski's original word *bit*. Though many actors use the words interchangeably, in this book, they will be given two different definitions.

There is folklore among acting circles that suggests the word *beat* became commonplace after Stanislavski spoke to an American audience and used the term *bit*. Due to the accent with which he spoke English, the word *bit* sounded like *beat*, and the Americans began to use that term instead. A second yet very similar variation on this story is provided by Richard Schechner in the book *By Means of Performance: Intercultural Studies of Theatre and Ritual*.

> The Russian emigrees [*sic*]—Richard Boleslavsky, Maria Ouspenskaya, Michael Chekhov—who first taught Stanislavski's system in America spoke with a heavy accent. When they said "bit" their students heard "beat." Beat seemed an appropriate musical metaphor, and so the new pronunciation stuck. But Stanislavski meant "bit," a term familiar to vaudeville entertainers as well as actors on the legitimate stage.[1]

Whether or not these stories are true is up for debate, and the debate is

---

1. Richard Schechner, "Magnitudes of performance" in *By Means of Performance: Intercultural Studies of Theatre and Ritual*, ed. Richard Schechner and Willa Appel (New York: Cambridge University Press, 1990), 48.

actually irrelevant. The two words, it seems, mean different yet related things. To understand the difference is to understand, first, what Stanislavski's original concept was.

In order to make the drama of a play (or opera) digestible, Stanislavski suggested dividing it into *units*, much like one would dole out portions of a large casserole among guests. The unit division, in Stanislavski's mind, occurred in the main points of the drama and not in the minute details. These could be scenes, acts, or larger. These large portions can and should be broken into even smaller units of action. Stanislavski used the word *bit* to represent the smaller portions of a larger unit. The bit was a portion of the larger work that could be isolated and still represent a complete thought or action. This is not unlike a sentence in a paragraph; the paragraph itself is part of a larger unit: the chapter, which is part of an even larger unit: the book. The sentence can be isolated and reworked for clarity within the paragraph and so on. However, the sentence, like the bit, must also remain a part of the larger idea.

In the division of a play or opera into bits, one trap is to overdivide. A singer or actor has to be careful not to divide the work into a frantic series of emotional changes concentrating more on large ideas and significant emotional shifts. Stanislavski suggested an actor determine the crux of the play or the essential element for which the play exists. Once the actor has determined that large dramatic point, he or she must find the *main* points of the story without concerning him- or herself too much with small details.[2]

The term *beat*, bandied about by actors and directors alike, often causes some confusion for singers. Actors and directors often remark, "There is a beat here," or as teachers sometimes do, simply scream the word "Beat!" in the middle of a scene. Of course when one doesn't know what that word means (in context) it can be disconcerting when someone screams it from across the room. The interpretation of the term becomes even more difficult when considering that the word *beat* is often used to define two different things—one, the entire bit or unit of action, or two, the beginning or ending of that bit. I have chosen to separate the two in the interest of clarity. This reinterpretation may be met with some distain in acting circles, but it seems necessary, considering the confusion with which the term *beat* is met.

It is likely that the terms *bit* and *beat* were used interchangeably at first. However, the unit and bit differ from a beat, and for the purposes of this book, I will define a beat in the following way: whereas a unit is a large

---

2. Stanislavski, *Prepares*, 109.

portion of drama divided into smaller actions (bits), a beat is the *point* at which one bit ends and another begins—or simply where something changes (see the illustration below).

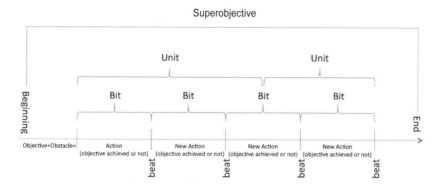

Illustration 9.1: Bits, units, versus beats. Objectives, obstacles, and actions will be discussed in the next chapter.[3]

Obviously in music, a beat is a measurement related to pace (tempo) and the division of measures into units (meter). Insofar as a beat is a point of division, a musical beat is similar to an acting beat and bit. In this analogy, the acting beat would represent the attack (as musical sounds have an attack [beginning], followed by decay, and finally release [end]). A play or an opera can be characterized as the most important event or events in a character's life compressed into a smaller unit of time (after all, if one were asked to sit through subtle emotional shifts for two to four hours, he or she would likely stay home). Characters in a drama or comedy travel through many large emotions during the course of their stage lives. Shifts in these emotions or in the character's focus occur when something changes. The vanguard of that moment is the beat.

Imagine you are sitting in a coffee shop staring blankly out the window when a former lover, someone you haven't seen since you parted, walks through the door (the beginning of the bit). At that moment, there is an unmistakable emotional shift. Whether or not you parted on good terms, you will likely experience a rush of emotion (positive or negative). At the moment this occurs, your previous emotional state ends and a new one begins. This moment of change constitutes a beat. To continue this scenario, imagine that your former lover, who left you abruptly and whom you have missed painfully, crosses the room and sits down next to you. You would

---

3. Illustration by the author.

likely go from one emotional state (e.g., surprise at seeing him or her) to another (e.g., panic as he or she approaches your table); you have completed a bit recognizable by the presence of a beat. Again, continuing in this scenario, after conversing casually for a few minutes, your former lover says, "I made a terrible mistake." The uttering of those words produces a third emotional change (panic to elation or confusion, for example); that again is the end of the previous bit and the beginning of a new bit with a beat in between. For Stanislavski, a bit represented a unit of action. This can be interpreted as a *complete* action—one that has a beginning, middle, and end. The previous analogy presents an example of the most detectable beat in a scene—when a character leaves or enters.[4]

As a bit is a complete unit of action, it is safest to define a beat as a point in which the bit changes. Beats are likely some of the most important elements in the portrayal of a character. The emotional change is the inner manifestation of a beat, but that inner change is always accompanied by a change in physical demeanor. An audience sees only the physical change, which indicates to them the inner emotional shift. For example, if in the last scenario, your lover enters and your emotional response is to panic, your physical demeanor would show that as erratic movement (perhaps a frantic attempt to hide behind a book). It is important to note that a beat is not only a place in which a character moves from one emotion to another, diametrically opposed emotion. A beat can also occur at a point at which a character's emotional state moves to the next level.

Consider for a moment the great artistry of Charlie Chaplin. Charlie Chaplin's success was in silent movies and was due to his uncanny ability to show emotional context on his face or in his body. With acting (as espoused by Stanislavski) in its infancy during this era, modern actors might look upon Charlie Chaplin and silent movies in general as being "over the top." However, if "acting" is truly "reacting," no one can argue with the ability of these actors to tell a story through physical action. A beat, in addition to being defined as a moment in which something changes, can also be defined as a moment that requires a reaction. The silent-movie actors of Chaplin's generation were masters at the action-reaction paradigm. As for Chaplin himself, it may be interesting to note that he was aware of Stanislavski and even used some of his principles in his own acting.[5]

EXAMPLE: "DIDO AND AENEAS"

In Purcell's *Dido and Aeneas*, the recitative "Your counsel all is urged in

---

4. Bella Merlin, *The Complete Stanislavski Toolkit* (Hollywood: *Drama Publishers*, 2007), 72.
5. Moore, *System*, 28.

vain" (No. 33) begins as an argument between Dido and Aeneas, eventually leading to Aeneas's departure and Dido's suicide. Looking past the fact that Dido is the Queen of Carthage and Aeneas a Trojan prince, this scene is simply a fight between a man and a woman.[6] With respect to the discussion at hand, Dido's emotional state does not change from one to another. She simply becomes more and more angry (or desperate). There is a steady crescendo of emotion from Aeneas's entrance until his exit.

AENEAS
What shall lost Aeneas do?
How, royal fair, shall I impart
The gods' decree, and tell you we must part?

DIDO
Thus on the fatal banks of Nile,
Weeps the deceitful crocodile.
Thus hypocrites that murder act,
Make heaven and gods the authors of the fact.

AENEAS
By all that's good,

DIDO
By all that's good no more,
All that's good you have forswore.
To your promis'd empire fly,
And let forsaken Dido die.

AENEAS
In spite of Jove's command, I'll stay.
Offend the gods, and love obey.

DIDO
No, faithless man, thy course pursue,
I'm now resolv'd as well as you.
No repentance shall reclaim
The injured Dido's slighted flame.
For 'tis enough whate'er you now decree,
That you had once a thought of leaving me.

AENEAS
Let Jove say what he will: I'll stay!

---

6. It is important for actors and singers alike to understand that human nature has not changed much in civilization. Though performers often portray characters of a social stratum they themselves may never reach (e.g., queens, kings, and so forth) or that may not exist (e.g., gods and witches), those that wrote these interactions were human and subject to the realities of human nature.

DIDO
Away, away,

AENEAS
No, no, I'll stay,

DIDO
away, away!

AENEAS
no, no, I'll stay,

DIDO
No, no,

AENEAS
I'll stay,

DIDO
no, no,

AENEAS
I'll stay,

DIDO
no, no,

AENEAS	**DIDO**
I'll stay, and love obey!	away, away, away,
I'll stay, and love obey, I'll stay,	away, away,
I'll stay, and love obey, and love obey.	To Death I'll fly if longer you delay;
	away, away!

Within this unit (beginning with Aeneas's entrance and ending with his departure), there are many beats and related bits. These beats or emotional changes are predicated on the words being uttered, the physical actions undertaken, and the reactions to those items. From Aeneas's first words of the scene, Dido's reactions grow more and more despondent. Each of Dido's angry outbursts leads Aeneas to an action. For example, in the following excerpt, Dido's anger reaches a peak, requiring Aeneas to change his approach. At this moment of change, there is a beat. This example is discussed from Aeneas's perspective only. Dido will have her own set of beats.

[Unit begins; bit begins]
[beat]

AENEAS
What shall lost Aeneas do?
How, royal fair, shall I impart
The gods' decree, and tell you we must part?

DIDO
Thus on the fatal banks of Nile,
Weeps the deceitful crocodile.
Thus hypocrites that murder act,
Make heaven and gods the authors of the fact.

[bit ends]
[beat]
[new bit begins]

AENEAS
By all that's good,

DIDO
By all that's good no more,
All that's good you have forswore.
To your promis'd empire fly,
And let forsaken Dido die.

[bit ends]
[beat]
[new bit begins]

AENEAS
In spite of Jove's command, I'll stay.
Offend the gods, and love obey.

[Unit continues until Aeneas's departure ...]

At the beginning of each new bit (at the point of the beat), there is a new action or a change in tactics. The bits' and beats' relationships to objectives and obstacles may also be seen in this in this excerpt. If Aeneas's objective in this scene is to console Dido, his attempt to console her by explaining his required task has been rejected, resulting in further belligerence from her. At the moment that this particular beat occurs, Aeneas abandons his attempt to reason with Dido and proceeds to reject his mission. These concepts will be discussed in detail in the next chapter.

Many actors, directors, and acting teachers may not understand the need for a distinction between bits and beats. They may reject it outright. After all, bits and beats were once the same. There is room for debate on this issue. However, it is difficult to argue that actions do not have a beginning, middle, and end. Therefore, it seems prudent to have a term that represents the space between the end of one action and the beginning of another. *Beat*, whether or not it was originally intended to be that, seems to have taken on that definition. Or perhaps it just fits the bill.

CHAPTER ELEVEN

Objectives, Obstacles, and Actions

In his System, no idea garnered as much significance or improved acting as quickly as Stanislavski's work on justifying physical actions. During the course of his life, Stanislavski abandoned the work on affective memory that had been so important and moved toward psychological motivation. Stanislavski believed that all physical actions are governed by psychological stimuli, and by relation, all needs or wants demand physical actions to be achieved.

Need: I am hungry.
Action: I scramble an egg.

Need: I want a paycheck.
Action: I go to work.

Stanislavski's system of acting, especially later in his life, was based primarily on what can be described as a system of objectives, obstacles, and the actions undertaken to achieve said objectives in the face of said obstacles. Perhaps best articulated in *Creating a Role*, Stanislavski referred to these motivations as *inner impulses* and later, *objectives*.

> I recall my morning visit to Famusov, when he was singing, and now I not only feel myself there with him, in this room; I not only feel the presence of a live object and sense his emotions; I also begin to be aware of certain desires, impulses toward some nearby objective. I wish Famusov would pay some attention to me. I seek appropriate words and actions to bring this about; for instance, I am tempted to tease the old man because I believe he must be funny when his dander is up.[1]

---

1. Constantin Stanislavski, *Creating a Role,* trans. Elizabeth Reynolds Hapgood (New York: Theatre Arts, 1989), 45.

This concept is fairly simple (even if its application is not). Humans (and animals) have needs and wants (objectives). Some of these objectives are easily attained, some are more difficult, and some are impossible. All objectives are accompanied by *obstacles*—that which lies between the objective and the acquisition of the objective. Fran Dorn, an acting teacher and friend, provides the following example:

> I want a dollar (objective) from Alan; Alan says "no" (I perceive as "belligerence"[obstacle]); I cajole (action) Alan. As long as Alan continues to say "no" in various ways, I will continue to do things to him until I reach my objective. The obstacles and actions are likely to escalate as I become more desperate to obtain my objective and the scene should be theatrically interesting as a result.

All instinctual behavior is built on this premise. Animals, for example, do not have the same capacity for thought as humans do, yet they act instinctively in order to survive. They hunt, hide, cover their tracks, or warn predators; their needs create actions.

Formal definitions of *objective*, *obstacle*, and *action*, provided by Robert Blumenfeld, are as follows:

> **objective** *n.* What a character wants; the character's **goal**; the character's aim; the **problem** the character has to solve; that towards which the character's motivation compels him or her to go; that which galvanizes the character into action. There is an objective for a beat (*beat objective*); for a scene (*scene objective*); for the play as a whole (*play objective*). Alice Spivak has innovatively and helpfully provided further categories of objectives: for a situation (*situational objective*); for a relationship (*relationship objective*); for the character as a whole (*character objective*; or *life objective*).[2]

> **obstacle** *n.* Something that is in a character's way, preventing the character from accomplishing an **objective**. It may be physical, another character, emotional, external, or internal.[3]

> **action** *n.* Something an actor/character does or says purposefully at a specific **moment** in furtherance of an **objective**.[4]

In order to complete the necessary analysis required to achieve Stanislavski's goal of a truthful performance each and every time, a performer must first

---

2. Blumenfeld, *Dictionary*, 185.
3. Ibid.
4. Ibid., 6.

understand and identify these fundamental elements of human behavior. These elements are common to most modern acting techniques and have become part of almost all dialogues concerning acting since the System was created. At their very base, they are meant to help the performer answer the question "Why?"—why does the character do and say what he or she does and says?

Actors from different circles refer to objectives in different ways. Those from the Stella Adler school of thought may refer to what she deemed "justification."[5] This can be somewhat confusing, as *objective* seems to refer to the motivation of a given action, whereas *justification* seems to refer to the reason for action (one proceeds the action and one follows it, respectively). In fact, they are essentially the same. In life, the objective for an action occurs before the action takes place, but we are rarely aware of the objective until after the action is complete. In the theatre, performers are often given actions or "business" to do and are required to justify it based on their characters' backgrounds and given circumstances. So essentially, they are the same. Stanislavski looked upon objectives as proceeding actions whether or not we are aware of them, and this understanding of the term is the most common.

Many interpretations and expansions have been made with regard to these elements. For example, an objective can be defined as what a character wants; however, it is sometimes beneficial to differentiate between what a character wants in a given moment (or *bit objective*[6]), what he or she wants for the scene (or *scene objective*), or his or her overall goal during the course of the play or opera (*play objective* or *superobjective*[7]).

Objectives are very closely related to the bits and beats discussed in the last chapter. Despite the need to divide the libretto or play into digestible bits that have their own objectives (bit objectives), the actor or singer needs to be able to connect those bits together in furtherance of the character's overall goal for the play. This connection is what Stanislavski called the *through-action*. For example, in *Il barbiere di Siviglia*, Dr. Bartolo's superobjective, or in Stanislavski's words, *supertask*,[8] is to marry his ward, Rosina. All of the actions Bartolo takes during the course of the opera are in furtherance of that objective. These actions create a line from the beginning of the opera to the ultimate success or failure (in Bartolo's case, failure)

5. Adler, *Technique*, 48.
6. The definition provided here is that of Blumenfeld's *beat objective*, but with respect to the previous discussion on bits and beats and in the interest of clarity, I use the term *bit objective*.
7. Larry Moss, *The Intent to Live: Achieving Your True Potential as an Actor* (New York: Bantam Dell, 2006), 19–20.
8. Benedetti, *Stanislavski*, 98.

of the superobjective. This line of actions constitutes Bartolo's through-action. Stanislavski believed that not only should actors know what their immediate goals are; they should also know what their ultimate goals are and how their actions fit into those goals.

When considering the problem of a superobjective, it is important to understand that a superobjective will present itself only after careful study of the libretto and source material has been completed. A performer's concept of the superobjective may change during the course of rehearsals as understanding of the character grows (sometimes aided by the insights of other performers and the director). However, the character's superobjective is not simply a justification for actions that a singer tacks on at the end of the process. A performer's choice of a superobjective will change his or her approach to the character. It is also important to note that ten different performers will interpret a character's superobjective ten different ways, and none of them necessarily wrong.

Consider the character of Don José in Georges Bizet's *Carmen*. Different performers would interpret him differently. He has been played as an innocent swept into these events by a wicked woman, a person desperate for love, and so forth. Understanding what motivates José stems from a detailed study of the information available—the libretto, obviously, and the works of Prosper Mérimée, including *Carmen*, *L'histoire de Rondino*, and *Letters from Spain*, to name just a few. One item that appears in José's past is the fact that in his youth, he committed a crime, was banished from his town, and following subsequent events, joined the regiment. When we meet José in the first act of the opera, however, he appears innocent and devoted to the regiment and the life of a soldier. Putting those elements together, one may conclude that a suitable superobjective for José, his goal in life, and the desire that drives him is "redemption." When we meet Michaëla, we find out that José's mother, whom he has not seen since leaving his hometown, has forgiven him. The significance of the crime that José has committed is that it shows his propensity for uncontrollable violence. In the Mérimée story (as well as the dialogue version of the show, but not the recitative version), Don José tells of a time in which he won a game of handball and was subsequently challenged to a fight (with *maquilas* or fighting sticks).[9] Don José only reveals that he won the fight, and that he was subsequently banished. It is widely believed that Don José killed his opponent in this fight, though neither the Mérimée story nor the dialogue version of the opera specifically says this. Nevertheless, this fact will help to explain

---

9. Mary Dibbern, *Carmen: A Performance Guide* (Hillsdale: Pendragon, 2000), 278.

Don José's rash behavior during the course of the opera (through-action), especially toward Carmen, as well as inform the superobjective.

With redemption as a superobjective, Don José's actions become much more understandable and interesting. "Redemption" answers the question, "Why does Don José want so badly to return to his regiment after going to prison for Carmen?" Redemption also adds an element of depth to the final scene of the opera, as his redemption no longer lies with the regimental life of a soldier but in building a life with Carmen—a woman for whom he has sacrificed so much. After all, since he has ruined his own life for her, to lose her then would mean his choices had all been wrong. There is even evidence of this in the libretto when Don José says to Carmen, "Ah! laisse-moi te sauver et me sauver avec toi!" (Ah! let me save you and save myself with you!) Further evidence of this superobjective may be found a few lines later. After Carmen exclaims that she loves someone else ("Je l'aime! Je l'aime et devant la mort même je répéterai que je l'aime!" [I love him! I love him and before death itself I will repeat that I love him!]), Don José responds, "Ainsi, le salut de mon âme; je l'aurai perdu . . ." (So, the salvation of my soul; I will have lost . . .).

As for Carmen, she has been portrayed as pure evil, whorish, aloof, and angry, and often with no perceptible driving force. Considering her lot in life as a gypsy, and information gleaned from the previously mentioned background material as well as others,[10] it may not be out of the realm of possibility that Carmen's superobjective is simply "survival." As mentioned earlier, superobjectives are subjective. However, survival makes Carmen's choices seem much less cruel, and to some at least, much more interesting. Survival certainly adds an air of complexity to Carmen (complexity is typically present in real life but often missing from singers' portrayals of operatic characters.) A superobjective that many people might find easier to work with (though less interesting) is "to be entertained." There is little in the libretto other than Carmen's actions and the performer's sympathy to lead to "survival" as a choice (though it would not be difficult to justify it). However, there is some evidence that "entertainment" might be viable. In act 3, during a conversation between Escamillo and José, it is stated that Carmen's love affairs rarely last six months (intimating that she becomes bored). A singer may question "survival" as a choice in favor of entertainment by simply pointing to the fact that Carmen chooses to become Escamillo's lover after losing

---

10. In her book *Bizet and His World* (Knopf, 1958), Mina Kirstein Curtiss suggests that Bizet's neighbor, Céleste Vénard, and her literary works may have, at least in part, inspired the character Carmen.

interest in José. However, in that action lies a powerful argument for "survival." After all, becoming the lover of Escamillo elevates Carmen to a status that provides her the means and comfort necessary for survival (namely food, clothing, and shelter).

The performer must be careful in picking a superobjective for his or her character, as this choice will inform his or her perception of the character's actions for the entire opera. It should also be considered that the events to unfold are not known to the character at the beginning of the opera. For example, it would be a mistake for a singer to pick "to save Carmen" as José's superobjective. José does not know Carmen until the midpoint of the first act, and there is little evidence that he is even aware of her existence. The same can be said of characters in other operas (e.g., the Governess and Peter Quint [*The Turn of the Screw*], Figaro and Count Almaviva [*Il barbiere di Siviglia*], Mimì and Rodolfo [*La bohème*]—the list goes on). Whatever the superobjective, it is a significant element of a singer's character analysis, as it will inform every choice the character makes.

In *Stanislavski's Legacy*, Stanislavski (through translator Elizabeth Reynolds Hapgood) describes the relationship of *objective* to *action* in the following way: "In each physical act there is an inner psychological motive which impels physical action, just as in every psychological inner action there is also a physical action, which expresses its psychic nature."[11]

THE "WHY" EXERCISE

A simple exercise for identifying objectives, obstacles, and actions is the identification of these elements in the singer's own life. Breaking down and cataloguing the "whys" of one's daily actions goes a long way in teaching this concept. This can range from the very simple identification of elements (e.g., I want to eat—there is no milk for cereal—I eat a banana instead) to the complex emotional (e.g., I want my girlfriend to be happy—I am making her unhappy—I leave her). A more specific exercise for teaching these concepts is as follows:

1. The singer or actor is to take one (1) six-hour period out of his or her life and write down every action that he or she completes. These descriptions should be simple (e.g., I sweep up broken glass).
2. At the end of the day, the singer or actor should look through the list and attempt to ascertain "why" these actions were

---

11. Stanislavski, *Legacy*, 21.

taken. For example, "I swept up broken glass because I want a clean floor."[12]

3. Out of each of those actions, working backward, the singer or actor should be able to navigate the objective-obstacle-action map (e.g., objective—I want a clean floor; obstacle—I broke a glass on the floor; action—I sweep the floor).

Simple actions are easy to understand. For example, eating a peanut butter sandwich is easily deciphered ("I am hungry, so I eat a sandwich"). Dissecting a period in which complicated emotional events occur is closer to the work that will need to be accomplished with operatic characters. "I cried at a movie" will likely need more investigation than simply "The scene was sad." Why the scene affected a person so much is the real point. "I missed my dad" is more of a *justification* than an *objective*. "I wanted to see my dad" could be the objective; the obstacle, "He died ten years ago"; and the action, "I cried." In this scenario, the movie is not the reason for crying; rather, it represents the given circumstance.

As mentioned earlier, it is often easier to justify an action than to work from the point of the objective. Objectives often seem oversimplified. Justifications, on the other hand, are often more easily worded but are just as often not as specific or even as accurate. "I cried at the movie because the scene was sad" is not as accurate or specific as "I wanted to see my dad, but he died ten years ago, so I cried." This will take some practice.

Simply being aware of one's motivation in everyday actions goes a long way to helping them decipher the clues in a libretto. A director often has his or her own ideas about where a character moves and why. It is up to the singer to find his or her motivation for such a move, and understanding the character's motivation is key. If a singer moves or completes an action "because the director said so," it will often appear that way to the audience. There will be little motivation and little specificity in the action or move.

POINT OF VIEW

A performer's *point of view* is a valuable but often neglected element of his or her approach to a character. Understanding how a singer's personal experience plays into his or her behavior as the character is of particular importance. If the goal of the performer is to play the reality of a scene, then the adage "My perception is my reality" cannot be ignored when studying

---

12. I chose a positive want ("I want a clean floor"). Most acting teachers will not allow students to choose negative wants (i.e., "I don't want to . . .") because they are difficult to play. Changing negative wants to positive wants will take practice.

and rehearsing a role. It is important for singers and actors alike to realize that most works of theatre are based in reality. Though a singer may have never been a queen or lost a husband, she may, after careful analysis, realize that Dido is simply a woman in love with a man. When they argue, the argument is simply a fight between a man and a woman set to music.

Developing a point of view is not something one needs to undertake. Everyone has one. Accepting a point of view (either yours or someone else's) is often not as simple. As is the case with people in general, performers are products of their genetics, upbringing, and circumstances. A performer should not ignore a point of view, and a director should not discount the performer's point of view. As is the case with all performing arts, however, there must be room for compromise.

CHAPTER TWELVE

Libretto Analysis

Analysis of the libretto is required for the performer to answer the questions necessary to understanding the character and therefore portray the character truthfully. The first step a singer must undergo in the preparation of a role is the exploration of the background material related to the opera. This includes reading the original source material (if applicable). For example, a singer preparing the role of Charlotte in Jules Massenet's *Werther* should read Johann Wolfgang von Goethe's *Die Leiden des jungen Werthers* (The Sorrows of Young Werther). However, it is important for young and seasoned singers alike to understand that the story being told in the opera's libretto is not necessarily exactly the same as that of the original source material. A singer is meant to tell the story laid out by the librettist and set by the composer. The information found in the source material is meant to fill in gaps in the libretto if necessary, or to give the singer information not found in the libretto but necessary for creating the depth needed to portray a particular character. This material is not meant to take the place of the information in the libretto. When a singer steps onstage to portray Charlotte in Massenet's *Werther*, she is portraying Massenet's, Édouard Blau's, Paul Milliet's, and Georges Hartmann's Charlotte and not Goethe's Charlotte. This fact should never be ignored. It is also important to note that characters of the same source material set by different composers and librettists also require an awareness of what the specific composer and librettist intended and should not be confused with that of others.

Reading the libretto itself is an oft-ignored chore. It is necessary to understand the differences between the characters and their circumstances in the libretto as compared to the source material. It is often easy for singers to forget that characters have a past—characters have memories, feelings, a life that existed before the events of the opera. Decisions about these details must be made in order for reality to flow from the character onstage.

If the singer is not fluent in the language of the libretto, a thorough translation of the libretto must be completed prior to this second step. Singers must understand that a translation found in album or CD liner notes, as well as the English versions (or any other languages, for that matter) found in the score, are not literal translations. Subtleties of the language are often ignored if these translations are accurate at all. The singer must know what each word means, what it means in context, and what the idioms mean. This may also require help and further research, as language structures from one era may not be the same as another (Mozartian Italian versus Verdian Italian, for example). Languages and idioms change over time, so it is often helpful to consult not only a dictionary but other aids, such as a collection of translations or other trusted guides to operas. Translation software has grown much more sophisticated over the years, and companies such as Google provide free online translation services. However, older texts may still cause problems and may require additional resources.

It may seem that understanding the entirety of the road in which the characters must travel would be counterproductive to true "discovery" or authentic reaction to the unknowns set in motion by each character's actions. This may be the single greatest reason that acting is called "acting" and not "being," and why it requires study and technique much like singing. The idea is to become as lost in the moment as possible (as per the earlier discussion of moment-to-moment work or being in the moment).

HAGEN'S NINE QUESTIONS OR SIX STEPS

The next step in the preparation of a role is answering certain questions about the character that will help the singer—and ultimately, the audience—to make sense of the character's actions. Uta Hagen's "Nine Questions"[1] is an excellent starting point for such in-depth character development. In this set of questions, Hagen breaks scenes down into the information most relevant to the events.

1. Who am I?
2. What time is it?
3. Where am I?
4. What surrounds me?
5. What are my given circumstances?
6. What is my relationship?
7. What do I want?

---

1. Hagen, *Respect*, 81–85.

8. What is in my way?
9. What do I do to get what I want?

The answers to these questions are not as simple as they may seem. "Who am I" does not simply refer to the character's name, but also to all of those characteristics and influences germane to understanding the character's actions. For example, a wealthy person will react differently to adversity than someone who lives on the street (consider how differently José and Carmen react to each other in act 1 and act 4 after their fortunes and social statuses are reversed). "What time is it" not only refers to the time of day but also the time of year, the period in history, and so forth.

Hagen's intent was to extract that information necessary to proceed in an informed fashion. With the exception of the first question, which is less scene specific than the others, the answers should be limited to single sentences, achievable objectives, and simple obstacles. In her book *A Challenge for the Actor*, Hagen refined these nine questions into "Six Steps."[2] The "Six Steps" simply condensed the information sought in the "Nine Questions." For example, "What are the circumstances?" grew to include "What time is it?" and other elements:

2. What are the circumstances?
   a. What time is it? (The year, the season, the day? At what time does my selected life begin?)
   b. Where am I? (In what city, neighborhood, building, and room do I find myself? Or in what landscape?)
   c. What surrounds me? (The immediate landscape? The weather? The condition of the place and the nature of the objects in it?)
   d. What are the immediate circumstances? (What has just happened, is happening? What do I expect or plan to happen next and later on?)

MORE QUESTIONS TO BE ANSWERED

Whereas Uta Hagen found that nine questions (and later, six) would suffice in the exploration of a character in a scene, others have created their own series of questions based on this idea. Larry Moss, an acting teacher of the most current generation, expanded Hagen's nine (or six) questions to twenty-four, breaking Hagen's questions down into more specifics and

---

2. Hagen, *Challenge*, 134.

arguably giving the actor more information from which to work.[3] Stella Adler did very specific work in the area of character background and even developed her own simple list of questions—who, what (referring to the character's action), when, where, and why (referring to the character's reason for being in a specific scene), or what she referred to as the "Five W's."[4]

If all of these attempts to codify analysis are taken into account, boiling all of this information down into that most necessary and yet remaining specific, the following ideas may be isolated as essential for thorough character research and scene analysis. Though each singer will find his or her own essential questions, the following questions must be answered in as much detail as possible:

1. What is my background?
2. Why is my background germane to the scene at hand?
3. What is my relationship to others in the scene?
4. How do my relationships and my background affect my behavior?
5. What do I want in life (my *superobjective*) at the beginning of the show?
6. How does my background inform my superobjective?
7. What are the *given circumstances*? What is happening?
    a. In the opera?
    b. In the previous scene?
    c. In this scene?
8. What do I want at the beginning of the scene (my *scene objective*)?
9. How do my background and my relationships with the people in the scene inform this scene objective?
10. Does my scene objective or superobjective change, and if so, how?
11. How does what I want in the scene affect my superobjective?
12. What are my *bit objectives*?
13. What are my *obstacles*?
14. What are my *actions* in furtherance of my objectives?

It is safe to assume (in most opera) that the stakes are high, though the degrees may vary (happiness versus life and death, for example).

---

3. Moss, *Intent*, 303–304.
4. Adler, *Technique*, 72.

EXAMPLE: *FIDELIO*

The benefit of such an analysis can be seen in the following example from act 1, scene 1, of Beethoven's *Fidelio* (Op. 72), a duet between Jaquino and Marzelline. *Fidelio* is an interesting case, as Beethoven's opera is based on a French libretto by Jean-Nicolas Bouilly rather than a novel or play.[5] There are often fewer details in such works than in novels or stories based on historical events (*Nixon in China*, for example). This requires that the performer make "educated guesses" when answering background questions.[6] Without evidence to back up specific choices, perception becomes reality. Others analyzing this work will undoubtedly come to different conclusions based on their perceptions. There is nothing wrong with this. The "truth" in these examples is only meant to be absolute to the performer analyzing the work.

The first character to be analyzed is Jaquino:

What is my background?

I am a healthy man of around twenty who is in a position of some authority and importance in a prison's hierarchy. I am lower middle class (I have worked my way up to assistant from custodian). I have little education. I think I'm handsome, rugged, but feel awkward sometimes, and girls don't get me.[7]

Why is my background germane to the scene at hand?

I am of marrying age. I want to marry, as all men my age should be married. My lack of education contributes to my awkwardness, and I don't know how to talk to girls.

What is my relationship to others in the scene?

Marzelline's father, Rocco, is my boss, and I am Marzelline's coworker. I have known her since I was hired. I have chosen Marzelline to be my wife, but I have not asked her yet.

How do my relationships and my background affect my behavior?

I have pined for Marzelline since I met her. I can't understand why she doesn't see what is right in front of her—why she is always looking for something better. My

---

5. There is some discrepancy on this point. Many sources call the original work, *Léonore, ou L'amour conjugal*, a libretto (for an opera written by Pierre Gaveaux). However, the original work, as described on its title page, is a "historical fact in two acts and in prose mixed with song." If the original work is not an opera, than the text does not constitute a libretto.

6. Some information about the given circumstances in *Fidelio*, for example, may be gleaned from a study of the French Revolution and the Reign of Terror—the backdrop in which Bouilly wrote the work.

7. There will be a temptation to write what the character cannot possibly know (e.g., "Marzelline is in love with Fidelio"). The singer's analysis should remain innocent of such facts.

persistence paid off and she became friendlier. That changed when Fidelio came. She seems to like him. He is smarter than me and more comfortable with women than I am.

What do I want in life (my *superobjective*) at the beginning of the show?
I want to marry Marzelline.

How does my background inform my superobjective?
I am conservative and believe in family. I think Marzelline should too.

What are the *given circumstances*? What is happening?
a. In the opera?
I am in love with Marzelline, the jailer's daughter. Leonore has dressed up like a man, Fidelio, and taken a job in the prison in order to rescue her husband. Marzelline has fallen in love with Fidelio.[8]

b. In the previous scene?
This is the first scene of the opera, but prior to this, Marzelline has been doing laundry, and I have been completing paperwork and various chores. I decided this morning that I would ask for Marzelline's hand.

c. In this scene?
I ask Marzelline to marry me, and she soundly rejects me.

What do I want at the beginning of the scene (my *scene objective*)?
I want Marzelline to accept my proposal.

How do my background and my relationships with the people in the scene inform this scene objective?
I have loved Marzelline since I met her. I can't see myself with anyone else. People would respect me if she were to marry me; I wouldn't seem so ignorant.

Does my scene objective or superobjective change, and if so, how?
They don't.

How does what I want in the scene affect my superobjective?
Marrying Marzelline is the beginning of my plan for the rest of my life. If I don't marry her, I will have to find someone else to marry (which isn't likely). I also won't be the obvious choice to take over the prison when Rocco retires.

---

8. This question allows the singer to discuss what his character does not or may not know. However, the singer should attempt to stay innocent of the facts in his portrayal.

What are my *bit objectives?*
To ask Marzelline to marry me, to get Marzelline's attention, and to convince Marzelline.

What are my *obstacles?*
Marzelline ignores me and rejects my advances, and people keep knocking at the door.

What are my *actions* in furtherance of my objectives?
I propose, cajole, guilt, scold, and even beg.

It is important to notice in these answers the use of first person ("I am") rather than third person ("He is"). As previously stated, it is important that performers work as if the events are not happening to someone else but to themselves. A similar analysis of Marzelline follows:

What is my background?
I am a lower-middle-class girl, the daughter of the jailer (Rocco). I am sixteen years old, healthy, attractive, but perhaps a little hard and disheveled from my work at the jail. I wash clothes for the prisoners. I have little formal education, but working at the prison has given me life experience beyond my years, and a worldliness not common for a girl of my class and age (we have prisoners from many different countries and backgrounds—I talk to them).

Why is my background germane to the scene at hand?
I have known Jaquino since I was thirteen. His lack of education and ambition to leave this jail do not fit into my plans. I want a life beyond this place.

What is my relationship to others in the scene?
Jaquino is my father's employee, and I have known him since he came to the jail. I consider him a friend and I like him, but my feelings go no further than friendship.

How do my relationships and my background affect my behavior?
I try to obfuscate and dodge Jaquino's advances because I don't want to hurt him. I know that he is easily frustrated, so being curt with him usually puts him off.

What do I want in life (my *superobjective*) at the beginning of the show?
A new life beyond these walls.

How does my background inform my superobjective?
The men in my life feel that I don't know my place, but I want to see what else is out there.

What are the *given circumstances*? What is happening?
a. In the opera?
Leonore has dressed up like a man, Fidelio, in order to rescue her husband, Florestan, from prison. I have fallen in love with Fidelio.

b. In the previous scene?
I am ironing and doing laundry (my job), and Jaquino is doing paperwork or something. I'm not really paying attention to him.

c. In this scene?
Jaquino proposes marriage to me (or rather, he tells me that he has chosen me as his wife and then pressures me to say "yes").

What do I want at the beginning of the scene (my *scene objective*)?
Fidelio.

How do my background and my relationships with the people in the scene inform this scene objective?
Fidelio is interesting and different. Not like the men that I am constantly surrounded by in the prison and at home. He is sensitive, caring, and genuinely interested in what I think. My father is stern, and Jaquino is boring. I want to see more in my life than prison walls and laundry. I become hostile to Jaquino.

Does my scene objective or superobjective change, and if so, how?
They don't.

How does what I want in the scene affect my superobjective?
Fidelio is passionate, intelligent, sensitive, and worldly. He could take me away from my mundane existence and men like Jaquino.

What are my *bit objectives*?
Deflect his proposal; get out of this conversation.

What are my *obstacles*?
Jaquino won't accept "no" as my answer.

What are my *actions* in furtherance of my objectives?
I ignore, argue, and finally harshly reject.

If this analysis is then applied to the opera (in this case, the first scene of the opera), a clearer picture of the situation begins to emerge. The following is the text and a translation of the first-act duet between Marzelline and Jaquino, "Jetzt, Schätzchen, jetz sind wir allein" (No.1).[9]

Jaquino
Jetzt, Schätzchen, jetz sind wir allein,
Now, sweetie, now we are alone,

wir können vertraulich nun plaudern.
we can privately now chat.
(we can now chat privately.)

Marzelline
Es wird ja nichts wichtiges sein,
It will really nothing important be,
(it won't really be anything important,)

Ich darf bei der Arbeit nicht zaudern.
I should at the work not hesitate.
(I should not dilly-dally at my chores.)

Jaquino
Ein Wörtchen, du Trotzige, du!
One little word, you difficult [girl], you!

Marzelline
So sprich nur, ich höre ja zu ... etc.[10]
Then speak just, I am listening ... etc.
(Then speak up already, I am listening.)

Jaquino
Wenn du mir nicht freundlicher blickest,
If you [at me] do not friendlier look,
(If you don't give me a friendlier look,)

so bring'ich kein Wörtchen hervor.
then I can get not a word out.
(I can't get the words out.)

---

9. Translation by the author. Stage directions in the score have been omitted as they are typically ignored by the director. Regarding translations, it is important to note their subjective nature. Two people will translate a line two different ways. The English translations of this and following texts have been "normalized" in terms of capitalization and punctuation. However, as the interpretive value of punctuation can be argued and there is almost no way to know if the punctuations were from the librettist or the editor, the punctuation found in the original texts (for this book, French, Italian, and German) have not been altered from the sources used.

10. Repeated text will be marked in this fashion, (" ... etc.").

Marzelline
Wenn du dich nicht in mich schickest,
If you do not to me send,
(If you do not say the words,)[11]

verstopf'ich mir vollends das Ohr.
stop I completely the ear.
(I will completely plug my ears.)

Jaquino
Ein Weilchen nur höre mir zu,
A little while just hear me out,

dann lass'ich dich wieder in Ruh'.
then leave I you again in peace.
(then I will leave you once more in peace.)

Marzelline
So hab'ich denn nimmermehr Ruh';
Or so have I for never again to rest;
(If not, I'll never get any peace;)

so rede, so rede nur zu.
so talk, so talk just away.
(so out with it.)

Jaquino
Ich ... ich habe ... ich habe zum Weib dich gewählet, verstehst du?
I ... I have ... I have for a wife chosen you, do you understand?

Marzelline
Das ist ja doch klar.
That is really [very] clear.

Jaquino
und ... und, wenn mir dein Jawort nich fehlet, was meinst du?
and ... and, if to me your "yes" is not lacking, what thinks you?
(and if you said "yes," what do you think?)

Marzelline
So sind wir ein Paar.
Then we are a couple.

Jaquino
Wir könnten in wenigen Wochen ... etc.
We could in a few weeks ... etc.

---

11. In his book *German Miscellaneous Opera Libretti* (Leyerle, 2005), Nico Castel translates this particular line as "If you don't fall in with my wishes," which would indicate some sort of idiom, as "wishes" and "fall in" are not literal translations of the German. This is a good example of why resources such as Castel's series of books should be consulted even if the singer has good language skills.

Marzelline
Recht schön, du bestimmst schon die Zeit . . . etc.
Quite nice, you picked already the time . . . etc.
(That's great! You are already setting a wedding date!)

[someone knocks]

Jaquino
Zum Henker das ewige Pochen,
To the Hangman [with] this eternal knocking!

Da war ich so herrlich im Gang,
There was I so splendidly started,
(I was off to such a good start,)

und immer, immer entwischt mir der Fang . . . etc.
and always, always escapes me the catch . . . etc.
(but something always gets in my way.)

Marzelline
So bin ich doch endlich befreit!
So I am really finally free!

Wie macht seine Liebe, seine Liebe mir bang,
How makes his love, his love me fearful,
(How his love makes me nervous,)

wie werden die Stunden, die Stunden mir lang' . . . etc.
how become the hours, the hours [for] me long . . . etc.
(how the hours for me become so long . . . etc.)

Ich weiss, dass der Arme sich quälet,
I know, that the poor [boy] is hurting,

es thut mir so leid auch um ihn, um ihn!
it makes me so sorry also for him, for him!
(I feel so sorry for him, for him!)

Fidelio! Fidelio hab'ich gewählt,
Fidelio! Fidelio have I chosen,

ihn lieben ist süsser Gewinn . . . etc.
him to love is a sweet prize . . . etc.
(to love him is a sweet prize . . . etc.)

Jaquino [*returning*]
Wo war ich? sie sieht mich nicht an!
Where was I? she looks me not at!
(Where was I? she's not looking at me!)

Marzelline
Da ist er, er fängt wieder an!
There he is, he begins!
(There he is, he starts up again!)

Jaquino
Wann wirst du das Jawort mir geben?
When will you the "yes" to me give?
(When will you say "yes?")

es könnte ja heute noch sein.
it could today still be.
(it could still be today.)

Marzelline [*aside*]
O weh! er verbittert mein Leben!
Oh woe! [Oy vey!] he embitters my life!

[*to Jaquino*]

Jetzt, morgen, und immer, und immer, und immer nein, nein . . . etc.
Now, tomorrow, and always, and always and always no, no . . . etc.

Jaquino
Du bist doch wahrhaftig von Stein . . . etc.
You are still truly of stone . . . etc.
(You are still truly made of stone . . . etc.)

kein Wünschen, kein Bitten, kein Bitten, kein Bitten geht ein.
no wishes, no pleas, no pleas, no pleas [move you].

Marzelline
Ich muss ja so hart mit ihm sein,
I must so hard on him be,
(I must be so hard on him,)

er hofft bei dem mindesten Schein.
he hopes at the faintest sign.
(his hopes are aroused at the smallest kindness.)

Jaquino
So . . . so wirst du dich nimmer, nimmer bekehren?
So . . . so will you never, never be convinced?

was meinst du?
what do you think?

Marzelline
Du könntest nun geh'n!
You could now go!
(You could leave now!)

Jaquino
Wie? dich anzuseh'n, dich anzuseh'n willst du mir wehren? Auch das noch? auch das noch?
What? to see you, to see you will you forbid me? Also that? Also that?
(What? You will not let me look at you? That too?)

Marzelline
So bleibe hier steh'n!
So stay here!

Jaquino
Du hast mir so oft doch versprochen . . .
You have to me so often promised . . .

Marzelline
Versprochen? nein, das geht zu weit . . . etc.
Promise? no, that goes too far . . . etc.

[another knock]

Jaquino
Zum Henker das ewige Pochen, zum Henker!
To the Hangman [with] this eternal knocking, to the Hangman!

Es ward ihr im Ernste schon bang . . . etc.
She was in all seriousness quite nervous . . . etc.

wer weiss, ob es mir nicht gelang . . . etc.
who knows, whether I had not succeeded.
(who knows, whether I was successful.)

Marzelline
So bin ich doch endlich befreit!
So I am at last free!

Das ist ein willkomm'ner Klang . . . etc.
This is a welcome sound . . . etc.

es wurde zu Tode, zu Tode mir bang . . . etc.
it was to death, to death [I was] scared . . . etc.
(I was scared to death . . . etc.)

PART IV

A NEW PROCESS FOR
ROLE PREPARATION

CHAPTER THIRTEEN

Preparing Auditions and Performances
based on the work of Franchelle "Fran" S. Dorn

Once a familiarity with the concepts from the previous chapters is achieved, a system of preparation can be established, allowing for a more fruitful analysis of the character and ultimately a more truthful performance. The following scene-study method devised by Fran Dorn is an effective tool for the preparation of scenes and arias for stage and audition. It also provides a process from which a singer can work in order to improve his or her presentation throughout the rehearsal process.

I was first introduced to this method in a Shakespeare class and immediately recognized its benefits. The fact that it is applicable to the study of opera with little to no adjustment is primarily due to the many similarities inherent in the performance of William Shakespeare's work and that of opera:

1. A predetermined rhythmic structure (in opera, the rhythm, tempo, and melody are controlled by what the composer wrote and by the conductor's interpretation).
2. A highly poetic use of language and structure.
3. Dramatic devices such as monologues and soliloquies (arias), and dialogues and ensemble scenes (duets, trios, quartets, and so forth).
4. A language unfamiliar to the majority of the receiving audience.

Due to these similarities, it is also true that the study of Shakespeare itself may present an excellent supplement for the opera singer attempting to improve his or her preparation of operatic roles.

Dorn's method begins with a "First Reading," which is defined by the following steps:

1. Acquire an "actor's notebook."
2. Read the entire play.[1]
3. Look up vocabulary with which you are unfamiliar.[2]
4. Eliminate any pronunciation problems you may have.[3]
5. If the text is written in verse, scan.[4]
6. Outline the plot for yourself and determine what part your character plays in advancing the story line.
7. Pay special attention to what other characters say to and about you—these are clues to your character.
8. Read all of the background material you can about the play, including but not limited to the historical period, the location, and the playwright (include other plays he or she has written).[5]
9. Learn to make notes on any images or ideas that come to you.

With regard to step 8 of the above process, it is important to remind singers that background materials (especially plays or novels from which the libretto is taken), though helpful in filling in the gaps often found in operatic libretti, sometimes conflict with the libretto. It is, after all, the story of the opera that the singer is telling, and when it conflicts with the source material, compromises must be made in favor of the libretto.

The purpose of this first reading is for the actor (or singer) to gain a full understanding of the text. A second reading is then undertaken.[6]

1. Construct a character's history. This should include, but is not limited to: your full name; date and place of birth; familial relationships; physical, psychological and societal upbringing; favorite colors, foods, pets, hobbies, and major events in your life. Be specific! You know everything about your own life. At best, you will be given only four hours of your character's life (and likely not four consecutive hours). You'll have to fill in the rest.

---

1. For the singer, this step involves reading the entire libretto and the original source material (if any).

2. For the singer, this step encompasses the translation process, both word-for-word or literal translations and an idiomatic version.

3. For the singer, this includes all issues of diction.

4. Blumenfeld defines *scanning* as "to go through a line or lines of verse, for instance in a verse drama, analyzing the meter and rhythm; hence, the n. scansion: the analysis of meter in a line or lines of verse" (Blumenfeld, *Dictionary*, 240). For the singer, this may involve speaking the text in rhythm in a hunt for clues left by the composer.

5. For the singer, this step includes research into the librettist and the original author.

6. Much of this material was covered in the chapter on libretto analysis. Some information, however, is new.

2. Determine your historical relationship with your partner in the scene.

3. Reconstruct what has happened immediately before the scene takes place—what is your offstage life? The scene does not take place in a vacuum.

4. Explore the "emotional baseline." What does the character feel at the beginning of the scene, and what does that feeling prompt the character to do?

5. Start your "left page." The left page is used for writing notes during the rehearsal process. Do not "fill in the blanks" at home! When you have transferred your scene onto "sides," the back of the preceding page will serve as the left page to the text you are reading on the facing page.[7] Divide the left page vertically into three columns and horizontally into "bits"[8] corresponding with the script on your "right page."

   a. First column: *Objective* of the scene—what do you want? Ideally it should be a "thing" and something your partner is capable of providing to or for you. It should be something small and tangible, and you should recognize whether or not you are in possession of it (e.g., a hug, a pat on the back, five dollars, the crown). You must decide on your objective *before* you meet with your partner for the next rehearsal.

   b. Second column: *Obstacle* for each bit—what gets in your way? At the end of each bit, you should rightfully have your objective. You don't (otherwise the scene would end). However, your partner gives you something else— perhaps you want it, perhaps you don't—but you're going to have to deflect or overcome it in pursuit of your real objective, which becomes increasingly more difficult to obtain. Note the obstacle as a noun or verb (it will probably be what you perceive as your partner's *action*— e.g., she's seducing me, he's ignoring me, she's getting under my skin, his smile).

   c. Third column: *Action* for each bit—how do you get what

---

7. Creating the "left page" in a score will be explained later in this chapter.

8. In this method, a *beat* is defined by Dorn as "a group of words forming a complete thought or simply a sentence. Something occurs at the final punctuation that causes you to start the next sentence. That tiny transition between 'beats' is where you are inspired toward your next 'action.'" Considering the earlier separation of the terms *bit* and *beat* and in the interest of clarity, I have changed the word *beat* to *bit* where appropriate.

you want? Always a strong active verb performed to or on your partner. It need not be literal. Use the words to perform the action and allow the body and imagination to participate. Examples: cajole, mother, belittle, elate. Your choices should be organic (i.e., you will get an impulse to do something based on what is happening in the moment). Try to follow the impulse without thinking about it. You need to write it down only if you wish to repeat it later. Remember that your job is to demand a response from your partner. The action should *never* include the words *try to*, *not*, *say*, *explain*, or *tell*.

NOTE: do not confuse *action* with *activity* (e.g., sweeping, pouring tea, tuning the engine).

6. Inner monologue: Occasionally, a character's thoughts are taken completely out of the scene. This can be an interesting acting choice, if the actor finds it organically—even if the playwright does not suggest it.

7. Impetus: what does your partner say or do that causes you to speak and/or act? (See *obstacle*.) Technically, it will come at the end of your partner's line.

Actors should proceed through the scene improvising one bit at a time, repeating it until they find something they want to keep. Make a notation on your left page under the appropriate "Obstacle" and "Action" headings, and then proceed to the next bit. *Always* run the preceding bits before moving on to the new one. There are *no wrong choices*. There are only choices and better choices. The only unpardonable error is to make *no choice at all*.

Objective: To elicit responses from your partner (i.e., *do something!*).
Note: The left page should be done in pencil. Things change.

The left page can be a very useful tool in analyzing a scene, whether it is applied to the work of Shakespeare or to an operatic scene. Illustration 13.1 (pages 116–117) shows the construction of the left page (blank).

Below is an example of a completed "Second Reading" of Angelo's act 2, scene 3, soliloquy from William Shakespeare's *Measure for Measure*. The first step in this reading is to establish a "character history." Answers to the important character questions are not always available in the text of the play, libretto, or background material. It is important to make informed choices, even if that means gleaning information from what is available or making answers up (as long as they make sense in the context of the script). For Angelo, a character history might be as follows:

What is your full name?
I am a Deputy to the Duke and, as such, am only referred to as Lord Angelo or Angelo.

When and where were you born?
Vienna, July 23, 1574.

Do you have familial relationships, and if so, what are they?
I am an only child. My mother died in childbirth and I was raised by a loving father who now lives outside Vienna. I speak to him infrequently.

What is your physical, psychological, and societal upbringing?
My father was a cobbler with little ambition who never remarried after my mother died. My father and I were strictly lower class. My ambition exceeded that of my father's as I looked to create a better life for myself. My father struggled to understand this ambition, my strict adherence to rules, and my disdain for those who did not follow rules. Religion was very important to me, as Catholicism offered the structure that I longed for. I was always small in my youth, so I was bullied relentlessly, and girls did not pay attention to me.

Other information: favorite colors, foods, pets, hobbies, and major events in your life?
Aesthetics are not important to me. I appreciate drab colors for their piety. I eat what is necessary and rarely drink wine. Art is decadent. I have no pets or hobbies. I spent my early twenties studying to be a priest, but became disgusted with the debauchery that priests, cardinals, and even the Pope enjoyed. I was kicked out of the priesthood for voicing my disdain, but did not leave the faith (because that would be a sin).

Step 2 of the "Second Reading" may be asked and answered in the following way:

What is your historical relationship with your partner in the scene?
The audience is the physical manifestation of my conscience.[9]

---

9. This may seem an odd choice given the "fourth wall" in theatre. For an actor, the audience acts as a sounding board and responder to the character's innermost thoughts. At the very least, the audience is the character's inner self personified. A certain amount of energy will be needed to convince or influence this externalized imaginary partner. Either way, choosing the audience as a partner will lead the actor or singer to externalized choices rather than internalized choices that could be small and dramatically uninteresting.

[Illustration 13.1]

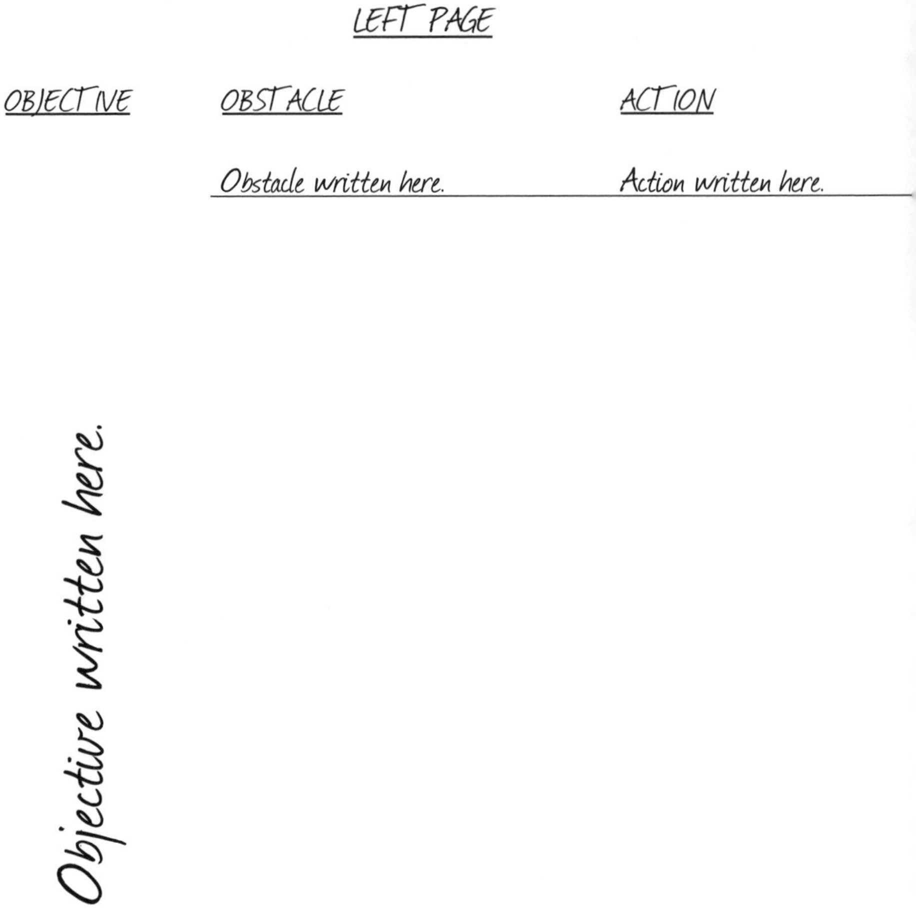

LEFT PAGE

OBJECTIVE *OBSTACLE* *ACTION*

Obstacle written here. *Action written here.*

Objective written here.

RIGHT PAGE

• Text of the scene on this page.

Step 3 is especially important in the process of establishing why the scene happens in the first place. This step of reconstructing "what has happened immediately before the scene takes place" is crucial in the performance of scenes and in auditions as it can inform the actor or singer how to begin. The most difficult beat[10] is always the first one, but depending on the circumstances, the first beat may be an extension of the previous scene (or the end of the previous bit).

What has happened immediately before the scene takes place? What is your offstage life?

I have just been visited by Isabella—a beautiful and pious young woman about to enter the nunnery—who came to beg for her brother's life. I have sentenced her brother, Claudio, to death for impregnating his fiancée. Isabella has asked me what she can do to change my mind. I told her to come back tomorrow and she left.

The last step undertaken before beginning the left page may be asked and answered as follows:

What does the character feel at the beginning of the scene and what does that feeling prompt the character to do?

I feel an intense sexual attraction to Isabella. I need to understand.

Illustration 13.2 (pages 120–121) shows the organization of the monologue into an objective, a series of obstacles, and the actions taken in the furtherance of that objective (or the left page). As a *soliloquy* is defined by the absence of another character in the scene (unlike a *monologue*, in which other characters are present), it presents the greatest challenge for the actor or singer—there is no one to react and no one to react to. In this particular example, as stated previously in the analysis, Angelo's struggle is internal. Though he has no physical partner, there is something to react to, be that his thoughts or the audience as his conscience. It is important to note that as these character choices are based on the actor's experiences (a main component of the Stanislavskian technique), it is highly unlikely that two actors would make the same choices. As Dorn notes in the "Second Reading" section, "There are *no* wrong choices. There are only choices and better choices. The only unpardonable error is to make *no choice at all*."

---

10. In this case, I use *beat* instead of *bit* for a reason. The point at which something changes is the end of the previous bit but the beginning of the new bit. This moment is sometimes difficult to find, especially in auditions.

An analysis of the first line of the soliloquy, as entered on the left page, illuminates the process. As previously noted, Isabella has left the room, and Angelo finds himself intensely sexually attracted to her, prompting the question "Why?" This powerful, amorous sensation leads Angelo to speak the words "What's this?" Angelo then repeats himself—a common element of operatic roles that singers often find problematic, struggling to motivate the repetition. Defining the objective and obstacle (as illustrated in the left page) provides a solution to this problem. It is important to note that the "Action" column is meant to represent external physical actions. Though motivations are internal, the actions must be external and strong. Strong and specific physical choices provide the most interesting acting choices. For Angelo, the strength of the physical actions must match the intensity of the obstacles.

The left page is meant, simply, to organize the thoughts of the character: the character has an objective; the character has an obstacle to which he or she applies an action; the character's obstacle either goes unresolved or is resolved in exchange for a new obstacle (to which the character applies a new action). It is important for the singer to understand that an objective is achieved only when the scene ends. However, in actuality, it may never be achieved.

As illustration 13.2 shows the soliloquy of Angelo, illustration 13.3[11] (pages 122–123) provides an example of the same process applied to Phillipe's soliloquy "Elle ne m'aime pas" from Verdi's *Don Carlos*. The only significant difference in the treatment of the two examples is that of the translation. For the singer whose fluency in the language of the work is not complete, it is necessary to translate the work (both literally and idiomatically) and work from the translation until the meanings are ingrained. The singer should keep in mind, however, that if he or she desires complete accuracy, he or she must work from the literal translation. Sentence structures in foreign languages tend to follow a different pattern, placing the operative words in different places than English, for example. It is also important to note that many operas were written before the modern form of the language. Italian, for example, was a language of many geographical dialects until the unification of the country in the mid-nineteenth century. It was only at this point that the Tuscan dialect was adopted as the official language. Given this fact, it stands to reason that operas written in Italian before 1861 (such as those of Mozart) would differ (in structure and idiom) from those of later composers. Idioms are

---

11. Translation by the author.

[Illustration 13.2]

LEFT PAGE

OBJECTIVE	OBSTACLE	ACTION
	My loins ache!	I tense.
	I am on fire!	Scream.
	I am seduced!	Breathe!
	The truth.	Blame her.
	She is so good.	Blame myself.
	"Why have I not felt this before?"	Psychoanalyze myself.
	Desire builds at the thought of Isabella's modesty.	Flagellate! [figuratively]
	My body tingles as I envision her naked body.	Slam arms on table!
	I do not recognize these feelings.	Pull out hair! [figuratively]
	My fantasy of her in my bed reappears in my head.	Mock myself.
	Sexual desire begins to win.	Throw up hands.
	I feel dirty.	Guilt myself.
	I feel my morality reassert itself.	Rationalize.
	I feel flush as I envision her eyes.	Accuse her of deceit.
	I am frustrated by weakness.	Warn.
	My resistance is fading.	Sit.
	My resistance is gone.	Collapse.

I want to resist my desire for Isabella.

RIGHT PAGE

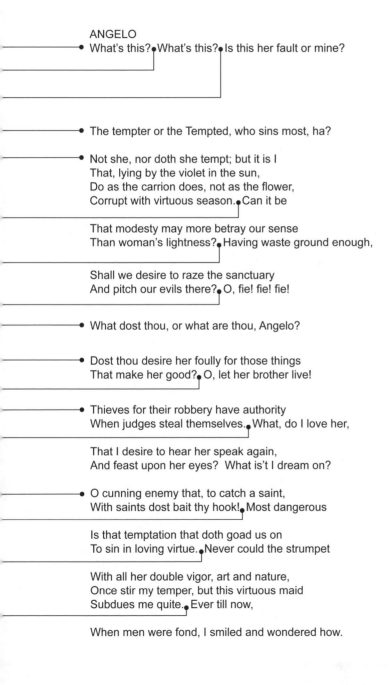

ANGELO
What's this? What's this? Is this her fault or mine?

The tempter or the Tempted, who sins most, ha?

Not she, nor doth she tempt; but it is I
That, lying by the violet in the sun,
Do as the carrion does, not as the flower,
Corrupt with virtuous season. Can it be

That modesty may more betray our sense
Than woman's lightness? Having waste ground enough,

Shall we desire to raze the sanctuary
And pitch our evils there? O, fie! fie! fie!

What dost thou, or what are thou, Angelo?

Dost thou desire her foully for those things
That make her good? O, let her brother live!

Thieves for their robbery have authority
When judges steal themselves. What, do I love her,

That I desire to hear her speak again,
And feast upon her eyes? What is't I dream on?

O cunning enemy that, to catch a saint,
With saints dost bait thy hook! Most dangerous

Is that temptation that doth goad us on
To sin in loving virtue. Never could the strumpet

With all her double vigor, art and nature,
Once stir my temper, but this virtuous maid
Subdues me quite. Ever till now,

When men were fond, I smiled and wondered how.

[Illustration 13.3]

LEFT PAGE

OBJECTIVE	OBSTACLE	ACTION
	My eyes are closing.	Rub head.
	My muscles are heavy.	Stand.
	I feel myself giving in to sleep.	Investigate surroundings.
I want to stay awake.	Sadness sets in.	Walk.
	Another night without sleep has passed.	Exclaim!
	The lack of sleep is winning.	Look out the window.
	I feel sick to my stomach.	Sit.
	My head is pounding.	"Sober" myself.
	Gravity is hard to resist.	Exhale.

RIGHT PAGE

PHILLIPE
Elle ne m'aime pas! Non! Son coeur m'est fermé,
She doesn't love me! No! Her heart is to me closed,

elle ne m'a jamais aimé!
she never loved me!

Je la revois encore, regardant en silence
I see her again, looking in silence

mes cheveux blancs le jour qu'elle arriva de France.
(at) my hair white the day that she arrived from France.

Où suis-je? Ces flambeaux sont consumés . . .
Where am I? These candles are burned out . . .

l'aurore argente ces vitraux,
dawn silvers these windows,

voici le jour! Hélas! Le sommeil salutaire,
here is the day! Alas! The (healing) sleep,

le doux sommeil a fui pour jamais ma paupière!
the sweet sleep has fled forever my eyelids!

Je dormirai dans mon manteau royal,
I will sleep in my mantle royal,
(I will sleep in my royal mantle,)

quand sonnera pour moi l'heure dernière,
when will sound for me the hour last,
(until my last hour rings,)

je dormirai sous les voûtes de pierre
I will sleep under the arches of stone

des caveaux de l'Escurial!
of the caves of the Escorial!

Si la royauté nous donnait le pouvoir
If royalty gave us the power

de lire au fond des coeurs
to read into the bottom (depths) of hearts

où Dieu seul peut tout voir!
where God alone can everything see!

Si le Roi dort, la trahison se trame,
If the King (is) asleep, treason is plotted,

On lui ravit sa couronne et sa femme!
They steal his crown and his wife!

typically difficult to translate regardless of the structure. It is sometimes advantageous to seek help in translations. Though there are many options available to assist in the task of translating, and Internet options improve with each passing year, an excellent resource in the translation of operatic libretti is the series of books by Nico Castel published by Leyerle Publications.

Illustration 13.4[12] (pages 126–127) is an example of the left page for an aria in which a second, albeit silent, character is present (e.g., a monologue as opposed to a soliloquy). In this example from act 3 of Massenet's *Werther*, Charlotte, who is married to Albert, has been reading letters from the man she actually loves, Werther. Sophie, Charlotte's sister, enters to find Charlotte upset and attempts to lighten her mood. As Charlotte grows more distraught, Sophie apologizes and becomes upset. In this example, though Sophie does not speak during the aria, she is present and reacts to what is happening in the moment. As stated previously, *acting is reacting*. The presence of a second character, silent or otherwise, creates an additional dimension—whereas in the soliloquy, all reactions are based on the actions or thoughts of the character, here a second character provides an active participant.

The left page for "Va! Laisse couler mes larmes" is also an example of the subjective nature of analysis (i.e., how the interpretation of a scene can differ from singer to singer and director to director). For example, this aria is often interpreted using an entirely different objective. Many singers and directors believe that Charlotte's objective is to "let go and cry." An examination of the libretto, however, points to the fact that Charlotte may be in tears before the aria begins, so the "let go and cry" objective would seem to be already achieved.[13] If the objective of the aria is achieved before the aria begins, there is no reason for Charlotte to sing the aria. Careful perusal of the libretto for clues and the singer's own point of view might lead to a different choice (e.g., the given objective for this example, "Comfort Sophie"). Once again, it is important to reiterate that there are no wrong choices and either objective can be justified. In fact, there are likely a few other objectives that may be appropriate.

Dorn's "Third Reading" allows the actor to reaffirm or change his or her choices, notating them on the left page. Before undertaking the

---

12. Translation by the author.

13. As translated in Castel's *French Opera Libretti Volume I*, a stage direction before the beginning of the aria states, "[Sophie goes] to Charlotte who is now in tears." (Castel, 1999, 47.) This direction does not seem to exist in any score. However, Sophie, upon returning to Charlotte, does notice that Charlotte is in tears ("Des larmes?").

third reading, the text should be memorized and the given circumstances solidified, including place, setting (time, weather, etc.), and surrounding environment (once again, the questions provided in chapter 12 are helpful in this step). The ultimate goal of this reading, according to Dorn, is to "create a physical world on the stage that is conducive to the life you are creating. The world must enhance your choices and not detract from them."

The final reading in Dorn's method ("Fourth Reading") allows the actor to bring the character into focus, answering the following questions:

1. What does your character wear and why?
2. What props, if any, does your character use? Are they personal or in the environment?
3. Does your character have any peculiar mannerisms, whether physically or psychologically caused?
4. Is your character like anyone you know or like an animal or machine you've seen?
5. What is your character's voice like and why?[14]
6. Can you observe any of these elements in your partner's character?
7. Make observations!

During this final reading, the actor is meant to work into the character, into the emotional baseline, and into the space, and locate the impetus for starting the scene. Remember that the most important beat in the scene is the one that precedes a first entrance (physical or vocal). The objective of this reading is to live organically as a three-dimensional character who honestly interacts with a partner from moment to moment toward the climax of the scene. This must be done in an agreed-upon fashion and in an atmosphere of mutual trust and reliance. In performance, the actor always knows where he or she is headed; the character never does.

For the singer, the first beat being the most important beat is a crucial point, especially with regard to acting in auditions. Often, audition arias (or aria sections) are preceded by long musical interludes. Motivating these interludes, staying in character, and finding the impetus for that first entrance is a difficult process. Though difficult, these are the most important acting moments in an audition or a scene. This will be discussed in detail in chapter 14.

---

14. This is not a question of voice type or fach; rather, it is a question of vocal characterization.

[Illustration 13.4]

LEFT PAGE

OBJECTIVE	OBSTACLE	ACTION
	I am in pain.	Release.
	Sophie is upset.	Look her in the eye.
	Sophie turns away.	Take her hand.
I want to comfort Sophie.	Sophie turns sadly to me.	Teach her.
	Sophie cries.	"Sister" her.

RIGHT PAGE

CHARLOTTE
Va! laisse couler mes larmes
Go! Let flow my tears;

elles font du bien, ma chérie!
they are good, my darling!

Les larmes qu'on ne pleure pas,
The tears that we do not cry,

dans notre âme retombent toutes,
in our soul fall again (all),

et de leurs patientes goutes
and with their patient drops

martèlent le coeur triste et las!
hammer the heart sad and tired.

Sa résistance enfin s'épuise;
Its resistance finally runs out;

le coeur se creuse et s'affaiblit;
the heart is hollow and weakens;

il est trop grand, rien ne l'emplit;
it is too big, nothing fills it;

et trop fragile, tout le brise!
and too fragile, everything breaks it!

The previous examples of left pages have been devoted specifically to soliloquies and monologues (arias). Illustrations 13.5 (pages 130–131) and 13.6 (pages 132–133) represent a set of "left pages" showing an ensemble, or in this case two characters in the same scene (duet). This scene (or partial scene), taken from act 3 of Puccini's *La rondine*, is an excellent example of how such an analysis would be undertaken for an ensemble. The given circumstance is as follows: Magda was the mistress of the wealthy Rambaldo. Despite her station, she has fallen in love with a young man, Ruggero. Magda has given up her life as a Paris socialite to move to the Riviera with her love. Unbeknownst to Magda, Ruggero has written to his mother asking her permission to marry Magda. Ruggero has received a letter from his mother and asks Magda to read it. In the letter, his mother gives her permission, happy that Ruggero has found a virtuous woman. The letter ends, "Give her a kiss from me." Magda is overcome with guilt, as the news of Ruggero marrying a woman of her reputation will ruin him. She loves him too much to ruin his life. Ruggero attempts to give Magda his mother's kiss. The text for the scene is as follows:[15]

[Ruggero attempts to kiss Magda.]

Magda
No! non posso riceverlo! Non posso, no, no!
No! I cannot receive it! I cannot, no, no!

Ruggero
Non puoi?
You cannot?

Magda
No! non devo ingannarti!
No! I must not deceive you!

Ruggero
Tu? tu? tu? tu?
You? you? you? you?

Magda
Ruggero! Il mio passato non si può scordare.
Ruggero! My past cannot be forgotten.

Nella tua casa io non posso entrare!
In your house I cannot enter!
(I cannot enter your home!)

---

15. Translation by the author.

Ruggero
Perché? Perché? Ah! Chi sei? Che hai fatto?
Why? Why? Ah! Who are you? What have you done?

Magda
Son venuta a te contaminata!
I came to you contaminated!

Ruggero
Che m'importa!
What do I care!

Magda
Ah! Non sai tutto!
Ah! You don't know everything!

Ruggero
So che sei mia!
I know that you are mine!

Magda
Tu non sai tutto!
You don't know everything!

Ruggero
Che m'importa!
What do I care!

Magda
Trionfando, son passata! tra la vergogna e l'oro!
Triumphant, I passed between the shame and the gold!

Ruggero
Non dirmi più! Non voglio! Non dirmi più!
Don't tell me anymore! I don't want [you to]! Don't tell me anymore!

Magda
Tu m'hai dato un tesoro, la tua fede, il tuo amore,
You to me gave a treasure, your faith, your love,

ma non devo ingannarti!
but I must not deceive you!

Ruggero
Quale inganno?
What deceit?

Magda
Posso esser l'amante, l'amante,
I can be the lover, the lover,
non la sposa che tua madre vuole e crede!
not the bride that your mother wants and believes [I am]!

[Illustration 13.5]

LEFT PAGE

OBJECTIVE	OBSTACLE	ACTION
	Ruggero tries to kiss me. [first beat]	Pull away.
	Ruggero follows me.	Push him back.
	Ruggero won't let me go.	Turn away.
I want things to stay as they are.	Ruggero won't let go.	Apologize.
	Ruggero doesn't care about my past.	Pull away.
	Ruggero's touch makes me weak.	Confess my sins.
	He stopped listening.	Hold him.
	He is in pain.	Take his hand.
	Ruggero's pain is palpable.	Look away.

RIGHT PAGE

MAGDA
No! non posso riceverlo! Non posso, no, no!
● *No! I cannot receive it! I cannot, no, no!*

No! non devo ingannarti!
● *No! I must not deceive you!*

Ruggero! Il mio passato non si può scordare.
● *Ruggero! My past cannot be forgotten.*

Nella tua casa io non posso entrare!
In your house I cannot enter!
(I cannot enter your home!)

Son venuta a te contaminata!
● *I came to you contaminated!*

Ah! Non sai tutto!
● *Ah! You don't know everything!*

Tu non sai tutto!
You don't know everything!

Trionfando, son passata! tra la vergogna e l'oro!
● *Triumphant, I passed between the shame and gold!*

Tu m'hai dato un tesoro, la tua fede, il tuo amore,
● *You to me gave a treasure, your faith, your love,*

ma non devo ingannarti!
but I must not deceive you!

Posso esser l'amante, l'amante, non la sposa che tua madre vuole
e crede!
● *I can be the lover, the lover, not the bride that your mother wants*
and believes (I am)!

E non sai che il mio strazio è così grande che mi par di morire?
● *And don't you know that my agony is so great that I feel I'm dying?*

Ma non devo più esitare. Nella tua casa io non posso entrare!
But I must not more hesitate: Into your house I cannot enter!

[scene continues . . .]

[Illustration 13.6]

LEFT PAGE

OBJECTIVE	OBSTACLE	ACTION
I want Magda to stay.	Magda rejects my kiss. [first beat]	Chase her.
	Magda pushes me.	Grab her.
	Magda turns away.	Turn her to me.
	Magda's sadness.	Reassure her.
	Magda pulls away.	Grab her.
	Magda's words are painful.	Turn away from her.
	Magda's touch seems so cold.	Demand answers.
	Magda's words are like daggers.	Make her stop.

RIGHT PAGE

RUGGERO
Non puoi?
• *You cannot?*

Tu? tu? tu? tu?
• *You? you? you? you?*

Perché? Perché? Chi sei? Che hai fatto?
• *Why? Why? Who are you? What have you done?*

Che m'importa!
• *What do I care!*

So che sei mia!
I know that you are mine!

Che m'importa!
• *What do I care!*

Non dirmi più! Non voglio! non dirmi più!
• *Don't tell me anymore! I don't want you to! don't tell me anymore.*

Quale inganno?
• *What deceit?*

Taci! le tue parole son la mia perdizione!
• *Quiet! your words are my perdition (punishment)!*

Che faro senza te che m'hai svelato quanto si possa amare?
What shall I do without you who to me has revealed how much one can love?

Ma non sai che distruggi la mia vita?
But don't you know that you destroy my life?

[scene continues]

Ruggero
Taci! le tue parole son la mia perdizione!
Quiet! your words are my perdition (punishment)!

Che faro senza te che m'hai svelato
What shall I do without you who to me has revealed

quanto si possa amare?
how much one can love?

Ma non sai che distruggi la mia vita?
But don't you know that you destroy my life?

Magda
E non sai che il mio strazio è così grande
And don't you know that my agony is so great

che mi par di morire?
that I feel I'm dying?

Ma non devo più esitare.
But I must not more hesitate:
(But I must hesitate no longer:)

Nella tua casa io non posso entrare!
Into your house I cannot enter!

The following example represents a section of an opera that most singers and opera fans would claim that they know intimately (as most have seen or even performed it) and do not need to analyze. However, there is much information to be extracted using the process that may not have been previously considered. In this example, illustrations 13.7 (pages 142–145) and 13.8 (pages 146–149) will show the application of the left-page technique to the first few pages of the final duet (act 4) of Bizet's *Carmen* (for Don José and Carmen, respectively). Illustrations 13.9 (pages 150–155) and 13.10 (pages 156–159) will show the last few pages for each character.

Below is the translation of the duet. The entire scene is provided for context. The lines have been separated, not only at the punctuation, but also where significant breaks in the singing line occur in the music. This will help the singer to transfer the information into the score by making the analysis of the rests themselves part of the preparation.[16]

---

16. Translation by the author.

No. 27. Duet and Final Chorus

Carmen [*short*]
C'est toi!
It's you!

José
C'est moi!
It's me!

Carmen [*without delay*][17]
L'on m'avait avertie que tu n'étais pas loin,
They to me had warned that you were not far,
(They warned me that you were not far away,)

que tu devais venir;
that you had come;

L'on m'avait même dit de craindre pour ma vie;
They to me had even said to fear for my life;
(They had even said to fear for my life;)

Mais je suis brave . . .
But I am brave . . .

et n'ai pas voulu fuir.
and did not want to flee.

José
Je ne menace pas . . .
I do not threaten . . .

j'implore,
I implore,

je supplie!
I beg!

Notre passé, Carmen,
Our past, Carmen,

notre passé, je l'oublie!
our past, I have forgotten [it]!

Oui, nous allons tous deux commencer une autre vie, loin d'ici, sous d'autres cieux!
Yes, we will both start a new life, far from here, under other skies!

---

17. This direction *sans lenteur* is sometimes translated as "not slowly." Given the immediacy of Carmen's line after Don José's response, "without delay" seems more appropriate and a more accurate translation.

Carmen
Tu demandes l'impossible!
You ask the impossible!

Carmen jamais n'a menti;
Carmen has never lied;

Son âme reste inflexible;
Her soul remains inflexible;

Entre elle et toi tout est fini.
Between her and you all is finished.

Jamais je n'ai menti;
Never [have] I lied;

Entre nous, tout est fini.
Between us, all is finished.

José
Carmen, il est temps encore,
Carmen, there is time still,
(Carmen, there is still time,)

Oui, il est temps encore . . .
Yes, there is time still . . .
(Yes, there is still time . . .)

Ô ma Carmen, laisse-moi te sauver,
Oh my Carmen, let me save you,

laisse-moi te sauver,
let me save you,

toi que j'adore.
you whom I adore.

Ah! laisse-moi te sauver . . .
Ah! let me save you . . .

Et me sauver avec toi!
And save myself with you!

Carmen
Non! je sais bien que c'est l'heure,
No! I know well that it is the hour,
(No! I know well that it's time,)

Je sais bien que tu me tueras;
I know well that you [will] kill me;

Mais que je vive ou que je meure,
But whether I live or whether I die,

Non, non!
No, no!

non, je ne te céderai pas!
no, I will not to you yield!
(no, I will not give in [to you]!)

José
Carmen! il est temps encore,
Carmen! there is still time,

Oui, il est temps encore,
Yes, there is still time,

Ô ma Carmen, laisse-moi te sauver, toi que j'adore!
Oh my Carmen, let me save you, you whom I adore!

Ah! laisse-moi te sauver . . .
Ah! Let me save you . . .

Et me sauver avec toi,
And save myself with you,

Ô ma Carmen, il est temps encore,
Oh my Carmen, there is still time,

Ah! laisse-moi te sauver, Carmen,
Ah! Let me save you, Carmen,

Ah! laisse-moi te sauver, toi que j'adore!
Ah! Let me save you, you whom I adore!

Et me sauver avec toi!
And save myself with you!

Carmen
Pourquoi t'occuper encore d'un coeur qui n'est plus à toi!
Why occupy yourself still with a heart which is no more yours!
(Why bother with a heart that no longer belongs to you!)

Non, ce coeur n'est plus à toi.
No, this heart is no longer yours.

En vain tu dis: "Je t'adore!"
In vain you say: "I adore you!"

Tu n'obtiendras rien, non, rien de moi,
You get nothing, no, nothing from me,

Ah! c'est en vain.
Ah! it is in vain.

tu n'obtiendras rien, rien de moi!
you get nothing, nothing from me!

José [*with anxiety*]
Tu ne m'aimes donc plus?
You don't love me then anymore?

[*with desperation*]

Tu ne m'aimes donc plus!
You don't love me then anymore!

Carmen [*simply*]
Non, je ne t'aime plus.
No, I don't love you anymore.

José [*with passion*]
Mais moi, Carmen, je t'aime encore,
But I, Carmen, I love you still,

Carmen, hélas! moi, je t'adore!
Carmen, alas! Me, I adore you!

Carmen
A quoi bon tout cela? que de mots superflus!
To what good is all that? What words superfluous!
(What is the point of that? What redundant words!)

José
Carmen, je t'aime, je t'adore!
Carmen, I love you, I adore you!

Eh bien! s'il le faut, pour te plaire, je resterai bandit,
All right! If need be, to please you, I'll stay [a] bandit,

tout ce que tu voudras . . .
anything that you would want . . .
(whatever you want . . .)

Tout! tu m'entends,
Anything! you hear [me],

tout, tu m'entends,
anything, you hear [me],

tout! Mais ne me quitte pas, Ô ma Carmen, Ah! souviens-toi, souviens-toi du passé! Nous nous aimions, naguère!
anything! But do not leave me, oh my Carmen! Ah! remember, remember the past! We loved each other once![18]

[desperate]

Ah! ne me quitte pas, Carmen, ah! ne me quitte pas!
Ah! Do not leave me, Carmen, ah! Do not leave me!

Carmen
Jamais Carmen ne cédera!
Never [will] Carmen yield!

Libre elle est née et libre elle mourra!
Free she was born and free she will die!

Choeur [*in the square*]
Viva! Viva! la course est belle! Viva! Sur le sable sanglant, le taureau, le taureau s'élance! Voyez! . . . etc. Le taureau qu'on harcèle en bondissant s'élance, voyez! Frappé juste, juste en plein coeur! Voyez! Victoire! . . . etc.
Viva! Viva! The bullfight is beautiful! Viva! On the sand bloody, the bull rushes! Look! . . . etc. The bull that [they] harass bounding rushes, look! Hit true (a good hit), right in the heart! Look! Victory! . . . etc.

José
Où vas-tu?
Where are you going?

Carmen
Laisse-moi!
Let me go!

José
Cet homme qu'on acclame, c'est ton nouvel amant!
This man who [they] hail, it is your new lover!

Carmen
Laisse-moi! laisse-moi!
Let me go! Let me go!

José
Sur mon âme, tu ne passeras pas, Carmen, c'est moi que tu suivras!
Upon my soul, you shall not pass, Carmen, it's me you will follow!

---

18. The irony of this line is that earlier in the duet, José tells Carmen that he has forgotten their past.

Carmen
Laisse-moi, Don José, je ne te suivrai pas.
Let me go, Don José, I will not follow you.

José
Tu vas le retrouver, dis . . .
You go to find [him], tell [me] . . .

[with rage]

tu l'aimes donc?
you love him then?

Carmen
Je l'aime!
I love him!

Je l'aime et devant la mort même je répèterais que je l'aime!
I love him and before death itself I will repeat that I love him!

Choeur [*in the square*]
Viva! Viva! . . . etc.

José [*with violence—violently*]
Ainsi, le salut de mon âme je l'aurai perdu pour que toi,
So, the salvation of my soul I will have lost for you,

Pour que tu t'en ailles, infâme, entre ses bras rire de moi! Non, par le sang, tu n'iras pas!
Carmen, c'est moi que tu suivras!
So that you can go away, vile [one], into his arms to laugh at me! No, by the (my) blood, you shall not go! Carmen, it's me that you will follow!

Carmen
Non, non, jamais!
No, no, never!

José
Je suis las de te menacer!
I am tired of threatening you.

Carmen [*with anger*]
Eh bien! frappe-moi donc, ou laisse-moi passer.
Alright! Strike me then, or let me pass.

Choeur [*in the square*]
Victoire! . . . etc.

José
Pour la dernière fois, démon, veux-tu me suivre?
For the last time, demon, do you want to follow me?

Carmen
Non, non!
No, no!
[sotto voce, with anger]

Cette bague, autrefois, tu me l'avais donnée, tiens!
This ring, another time, you to me had given, here!
(This ring, once, you had given me, here!)

José
Eh bien! damnée!
All right! damned one!

Choeur
Toréador, en garde! . . . etc.

[José stabs Carmen]

José
Vous pouvez m'arrêter.
You can arrest me.

C'est moi qui l'ai tuée!
It is I who killed her!

Ah! Carmen! ma Carmen adorée!
Ah! Carmen! My Carmen adored!
(Ah! Carmen! My precious Carmen!)

In the following illustrations, note the placement of the beat in these examples as represented by the dot at the end of the long line ("•"). Action is immediate at these points.

These examples represent the beginning of the rehearsal process. It is important to remember that the left page is a constantly evolving tool that, as rehearsals progress, will continue to gain focus. The completion of all four "readings" represents a significant analysis of the character and scene. As the director's vision for the show and the needs of the conductor are added to the process during rehearsals, the singer's choices may be adjusted. Though flexibility in the rehearsal process is a must, it is important that the singer comes to the first rehearsal with ideas.

Illustrations 13.7, 13.8, 13.9, and 13.10 (pages 142–159) include excerpts from the final scene of *Carmen* (*Carmen* by G. Bizet [New York: Schirmer, 1923, 373–374, 389–391]).

[Illustration 13.7a]

LEFT PAGE

OBJECTIVE	OBSTACLE	ACTION
		Approach her
	She is angry.	slowly.

Scene: I want Carmen back.

Superobjective: I want to redeem myself.

No 27. Duet and final Chorus.

[Illustration 13.7b]

LEFT PAGE

OBJECTIVE	OBSTACLE	ACTION
	She thinks I am here to kill her.	Back off.
	She won't look at me.	Cajole.
	She still won't look at me.	Touch her.

Scene: I want Carmen back.

Superobjective: I want to redeem myself.

[Illustration 13.8a]

LEFT PAGE

OBJECTIVE	*OBSTACLE*	*ACTION*
	He doesn't speak.	Break the silence.
	I am frightened.	Strengthen.

Scene: I want to be free of DJ.
Superobjective: I want to survive.

| | He does not respond. | Laugh at the danger. |

Nº 27. Duet and final Chorus.

[Illustration 13.8b]

LEFT PAGE

OBJECTIVE   OBSTACLE   ACTION

He does not respond.   Defy.

Scene: I want to be free of DJ.

Superobjective: I want to survive.

His touch scares me.   Get away from him.

[Illustration 13.9a]

<u>LEFT PAGE</u>

<u>OBJECTIVE</u>   <u>OBSTACLE</u>   <u>ACTION</u>

                       She will not budge.   Scare her.

Scene: I want Carmen back.

Superobjective: I want to redeem myself.

                       I am full of rage!   Hold myself back.

[Illustration 13.9b]

LEFT PAGE

OBJECTIVE   OBSTACLE   ACTION

She is leaving.   STOP HER!

Scene: I want Carmen back.

Superobjective: I want to redeem myself.

(Carmen attempts to escape, but Don José catches up with her at the entrance of the amphitheatre; he stabs her; she falls, and dies.)

[Illustration 13.9c]

LEFT PAGE

OBJECTIVE	OBSTACLE	ACTION
	I killed Carmen.	Repent.

Scene: I want Carmen back.

Superobjective: I want to redeem myself.

[Illustration 13.10a]

<u>LEFT PAGE</u>

<u>OBJECTIVE</u>   <u>OBSTACLE</u>   <u>ACTION</u>

Scene: I want to be free of D).
Superobjective: I want to survive.

He will not leave.   Hurt him.

[Illustration 13.10b]

LEFT PAGE

OBJECTIVE   OBSTACLE   ACTION

Scene: I want to be free of DJ.
Superobjective: I want to survive.

He won't take "no" for an answer.   Leave.

CHAPTER FOURTEEN

The Process and Recitative

R ecitative (*récitative* or *recitativo*) is an often neglected part of the learning process in opera, and yet one of the most important aspects of the libretto. Voice teachers rarely spend time in voice lessons working on the technique of performing recitative. Though the underlying reasons are not necessarily germane to this discussion, if we consider the following generalized axiom, some sense can be made of a voice teacher's priorities: *Arias and ensembles move the music forward;* recitativo *moves the story forward.* In other words, as voice teachers concern themselves more with the technique of sound and less with issues of drama, it stands to reason that recitative would not be as high a priority.

To scratch the surface is to write volumes on the study and performance of recitative. Though declamatory singing styles existed long before opera (e.g., incantation of Jewish prayer and chant in the early Christian church) and exist in many variations, this chapter will simply provide some clues on how to begin the process by focusing on the *recitativo secco* (or "dry," accompanied by continuo) and *recitativo accompagnato* or *stromentato* (accompanied by orchestra), and specifically, the recitative of Mozart.

MOVING THE DRAMA FORWARD

Consider how much information is disseminated—as a percentage of the whole—in a Mozart *recitativo secco* as opposed to an aria or ensemble. There is little to no repetition of text in recitative as opposed to a typical da capo aria. Also, the simplification of the underlying music, and maximization of rhythmic subdivision (specifically in *recitativo secco*) allows for, simply put, many more words to be intoned in a very short amount of time.

Musically, recitative is often melodically and harmonically easier to decipher. Despite the occasional harmonic curveball, there are few surprises. Again, considering the earlier axiom, this stands to reason as the progression of the drama is of highest import in *recitativo secco*. Take for example the following section of the recitative that precedes "Là ci darem" in Mozart's *Don Giovanni*.

Illustration 14.1: Excerpt from "Alfin siam liberati, Zerlinetta" (*Don Giovanni* by W. A. Mozart [New York: Schirmer, 1900, 61]).

The key of "Là ci darem" is A major, and though there are no sharps in the key signature of the recitative, this section is clearly establishing the key of A major (actually, the entire recitative is firmly establishing the key of A major after the preceding aria, "Ho capito," cadences in the key of F major). This is evidenced by the following progression beginning on beat 4 of the first measure:[1]

$$A: \quad V_2^4 \quad V_5^6/IV \quad IV \quad V_2^4 \quad V^7 \quad I$$

This is not an extraordinary cadential progression for the eighteenth century, nor would it be atypical in opera to this point in history and into the early nineteenth century. It is also, arguably, not particularly interesting harmonically. It was likely not meant to be. This is simply a musical roadmap from point A to point B that simultaneously moves the story along and informs the audience.

Though not harmonically interesting, the relationship between rhythm and tempo in recitative is often very interesting. If you took your favorite recording of any Mozart opera and followed the score while listening, you

---

1. Though the underlying chord in measure 2 could be called a I[6], the presence of a G♮ in measure 3 and the landing point of IV leads me to believe that this is a secondary dominant. Theorists may disagree with me on this point.

would realize that what is sung seems to only slightly resemble (with regard to the temporal relationship[2]) what is on the page. If you then attempted to sing *recitativo secco* as it is on the page, you would likely find it unnatural and boring, and the text difficult to follow. Composers surrendered a large portion of the dramatic responsibility in recitative to the singer (and the harpsichordist whose embellishments accentuate the text). It is not that composers were inept, they were simply working within a system of rules (specifically, rhythmic notation). This system of rules, though good, is not perfect. If a composer attempted to write natural conversation in recitative form, the resulting music would likely be so complicated as to require a singer to devote an inordinate amount of his or her time to its study.

It is the dramatic intent, the stresses of the language, and the underlying emotions that drive the pacing, articulation, and even dynamics in *recitativo secco*. For example, below is another recitative from *Don Giovanni* in which Zerlina and Masetto, a recently married couple, are arguing over the fact that Zerlina was nearly seduced by Giovanni only minutes after their wedding.

Illustration 14.2: Excerpt from "Masetto, senti un po'!" (*Don Giovanni* by W. A. Mozart [New York: Schirmer, 1900, 104]).

---

2. The *temporal relationship* refers to the relationship of tempo to rhythm. For example, if a tempo changes in the middle of a phrase or even note value (either a sung note or a rest), it may seem as if the rhythm itself has changed. This temporal relationship is what is generally referred to in this chapter as "pacing."

The drama in this excerpt is charged with anger on the part of Masetto and pleading on the part of Zerlina. The translation is as follows:[3]

Zerlina
Masetto: senti un po'!
Masetto: listen a little!
(Masetto: listen a moment!)

Masetto, dico!
Masetto, I say [to you]!
(Masetto, I tell you!)

Masetto
Non mi toccar!
Don't touch me!

Zerlina
Perchè?
Why?

Masetto
Perchè mi chiedi? Perfida! Il tatto sopportar dovrei d'una man infedele?
Why, you ask me? Wicked [girl]! The touch must I suffer of a hand unfaithful?
(Why, you ask me? Wicked [girl]! I must suffer the touch of an unfaithful hand?)

This sounds like an argument—one which could take place present day. However, it would be nearly impossible to reconcile the text with the music as it is written on the page. The pacing of such a recitative will be informed by the dramatic intent (not unlike iambic pentameter in the plays of Shakespeare— rarely do we hear the short–long/short–long/short–long/short–long/short– long of iambic pentameter when we see Shakespeare in the theatre or on film).

The flexibility afforded the singer in *recitativo secco* is largely the closest thing in opera to the spoken dialogue of a play, musical, *opéra comique*, or operetta. It offers the singer a more direct path from internal motivation to physicalization as he or she assumes more control over the elements of common speech (pace, dynamics, stress). For example, in reality, people typically speak much faster, more percussively, louder, and more erratically when angry; when sorrowful or apologetic, slower and softer. These are, of course, drastic oversimplifications. However, there are commonalities in the vocalization of emotions that can be found through observation of human behavior.

Recitativo accompagnato or *stromentato*, on the other hand, is not as flexible and is sometimes referred to as *misurato* (or *measured*), indicating the formally composed nature of the music (requiring a conductor). Dramatically,

---

3. Translation by the author.

recitativo accompagnato falls somewhere between arias and *recitativo secco*. *Recitativo accompagnato* may even contain sections of *recitativo secco*—for example, the third system, second bar, third beat of Illustration 14.3 from "Don Ottavio, son morta!" (No. 10a, *Don Giovanni*) in which Donna Anna tells the story of the event that led to her father's death.

Illustration 14.3: Excerpt from "Don Ottavio, son morta!" (*Don Giovanni* by W. A. Mozart [New York: Schirmer, 1900, 86]).

Though *recitativo secco* and *recitativo accompagnato* are differently challenging, the process for dissecting the text and applying objectives, actions, and obstacles to that text is the same as covered in previous chapters. Applying the "left page" to the study of recitative is not unlike any other operatic convention. In fact, it is often easier, as there is less repetition of text and shorter musical interludes. An example of such a left page can be found below, utilizing the following *recitativo accompagnato* from *Le nozze di Figaro*.

Hai già vinta la causa[4]

Il Conte Almaviva
Hai già vinta la causa!
You have already won the case!

Cosa sento!
What do I hear?

In qual laccio io cadea!
Into what trap did I fall!

Perfidi!
Traitors!

Io voglio . . .
I want . . .

io voglio di tal modo punirvi . . .
I want in such a way to punish you . . .

a piacer mio la sentenza sarà . . .
to my pleasure the sentence will be . . .
(I will decide your punishment . . .)

Ma s'ei pagasse la vecchia pretendente?
But if he paid the old [woman] claimant[5]?
(But what if he pays the old woman back?)

Pagarla!
Pay her!

In qual maniera?
In what manner?
(How?)

---

4. Translation by the author.
5. *Pretendente* is sometimes translated as "pretender," but given the context, "claimant" makes more sense, considering the legal case brought by Marcellina against Figaro in the opera.

E poi v'è Antonio, che a un incognito[6] Figaro ricusa di dare una nipote in matrimonio.
And then there is Antonio that to an unknown Figaro refuses to give a niece in marriage.
(And then there is Antonio who refuses to marry his niece to a nobody like Figaro.)

Coltivando l'orgoglio di questo mentecatto . . .
Cultivating the pride of this fool . . .

Tutto giova a un raggiro . . .
Everything requires a trick . . .

il colpo è fatto!
the blow is made!
(the deed is done!)

Illustration 14.4 (pages 168–169) represents the "left page" for this recitative.

FROM RECITATIVE TO ARIA: AN EMOTIONAL JOURNEY

One of the most difficult and consistent problems singers experience (especially in auditions) is the problem of connecting the recitative or introductory material to the aria when there is a long musical interlude (more than a simple cadence). In production, a director will typically give the singer stage business to fill up the introduction or interlude, helping the singer to bridge the music without seeming lost (this is not always the case, but it is more times than not).

In auditions, musical interludes can sometimes be the most painful moments to watch, especially if the singer has not made clear decisions about what should be happening, what the character wants or needs, or what the character is thinking. Singers sometimes fail to realize that the character is on an emotional journey throughout the piece and the introduction or interlude is always *part* of that journey. The absence of text does not mean the absence of thoughts or emotions. Consider this moment in the score a long bit, replete with a beat at both ends.

Illustration 14.5 is an example of such a moment from "Una voce poco fa." At the end of the introduction, there is a long interlude (twelve measures). Though not technically a recitative (instead, a *cavatina*), the long interlude exhibits the same characteristic problem associated with interludes between recitatives and arias.

In a production of *Il barbiere di Siviglia*, Rosina would typically be given stage business during this interlude. In an audition, a singer is not simply allowed to stop acting because there are no production elements. What does

---

6. *Incognito* is often translated as "unknown," which could mean "a nobody like" or which could also refer to the fact that no one knows (at this point in the opera) who Figaro's parents are.

[Illustration 14.4]

<u>LEFT PAGE</u>

<u>OBJECTIVE</u>	<u>OBSTACLE</u>	<u>ACTION</u>
	Susanna and Figaro think they have won.	Shake my head.
	I am embarrassed.	Pound the table.
	They seem confident.	Bark!
I want control.	I don't know their plan.	Figure it out.
	I need my own plan.	List assets.
	I need a clearer plan.	Talk it out.
	It's coming into focus, but still not there.	Think harder!
	I need to show them who is boss.	Declare war!

RIGHT PAGE

IL CONTE ALMAVIVA
Hai già vinta la causa! cosa sento! In qual laccio io cadea!
——• *You have already won the case! What do I hear? Into what*
trap did I fall!

Perfidi! io voglio . . . io voglio di tal modo punirvi . . .
——• *Traitors! I want . . . I want in such a way to punish you . . .*

a piacer mio la sentenza sarà . . .
——• *To my pleasure the sentence will be . . .*
(I will decide your punishment . . .)

Ma s'ei pagasse la vecchia pretendente? Pagarla! in qual
maniera?
——• *But if he paid the old [woman] claimant? Pay her! In what*
manner?
(But what if he pays the old woman back? Pay her! How?)

E poi v'è Antonio, che a un incognito Figaro ricusa di dare una
nipote in matrimonio.
——• *And then there is Antonio, that to an unknown Figaro refuses*
to give a niece in marriage.
(And then there is Antonio, who refuses to marry his niece to a
nobody like Figaro.)

Coltivando l'orgoglio di questo mentecatto . . .
——• *Cultivating the pride of this fool . . .*

tutto giova a un raggiro . . .
——• *Everything requires a trick . . .*

il colpo è fatto!
——• *the blow is made!*
(the deed is done!)

the singer do to fill this time without props or a set? Firstly, it is important for the singer to understand what the stage business would be. In the case of "Una voce poco fa," for example, Rosina would typically (in performance) use this time to write a note that she later gives to Figaro to deliver to Lindoro (Almaviva in disguise). However, when auditioning with this aria, singers are not advised to pantomime the action of writing a note. It simply looks silly.

Auditions are especially problematic for singers, as they often struggle with the question "How much acting is too much acting?" Pantomiming props or actions that involve props (such as writing a letter, drinking from a cup, and so forth) is rarely a good idea in an audition. However, it can be tricky when the item is germane to the story and specifically referenced in the recitative or aria. Consider the introduction preceding Valentin's aria from *Faust*, "Avant de quitter ces lieux." The first words of the edited audition aria are "O sainte médaille, qui me viens de ma sœur." This line specifically refers to a medallion that Valentin's sister has given him and from which he will now ask protection. Should the baritone pantomime the medal while singing this line, or bring a medal to hold during the audition? It is safe to assume that directors and conductors are more interested in seeing that the singer knows what he is saying. This is not an answer per se. There may not be a simple answer to this conundrum. However, the acting in auditions should be "just enough" to show the audition panel that the singer knows what is going on and has made specific choices (minus the pantomiming).

As mentioned earlier in this chapter, volumes could be written on the subject of recitative. Learning to perform recitative and learning to see recitative as an instrument of drama is paramount to being a good singing actor, especially with regard to Mozart. To this end, finding a good vocal coach who understands the language and has a firm grasp on the dramatic intent of recitative will go a long way in the learning process toward becoming a proficient singer and actor of recitative.

Illustration 14.5: Excerpt from "Una voce poco fa" (*Il barbiere di Siviglia* by G. Rossini [New York: Schirmer, 1900, 77–78]).

CHAPTER FIFTEEN

"Being" the Third Girl from the Left—
Acting for Choristers

The chorus is an integral part of the music in opera but is also, in most productions, an integral dramatic element as well. Despite this importance, there is really no such thing as a full-time professional chorister. Chorus staging is often limited to a five or six frantic rehearsals per production. Professional choristers are typically singers who have "day jobs" and perform in opera choruses for extra income, as a social outlet, or simply because they love the art form and wish to be involved. Some of these singers have advanced degrees in singing, some do not, and few are using the chorus as a stepping stone to principal artist or a professional singing career. For these reasons and others, there is often a feeling among choristers that the chorus is not a particularly important dramatic element, and thus, chorus "acting" is not that important.

There are choristers, however, who are professional singers or professional young artists, and their time in the chorus may lead to comprimario roles and more. Some summer festivals even compose their choruses completely of young artists working toward careers as professional singers. The ability of such singers to act is important to their career prospects but is also an important component of storytelling for the opera itself. Choruses are important. Consider the second acts of both *La bohème* and *La rondine,* which are essentially comprised completely of chorus music. The choruses in *Carmen* are characters unto themselves, comprising the actions of the townspeople, soldiers, gypsies, and spectators. Without these choruses, a significant element of these operas would be lost.

Recalling the previous discussion of early opera and its connection to Greek theatre, it is reasonable to assume that opera choruses retained some of the importance that the Greek chorus enjoyed. Greek choruses were meant to add significance to the story being told by providing commentary or narration. Some operas even use choruses not only in the spirit of Greek theatre but also in its execution (e.g., *The Rape of Lucretia* by Benjamin

Britten—in which the characters of Male Chorus and Female Chorus both narrate and comment on the events taking place in the opera—and *Oedipus Rex* by Igor Stravinsky, to name a couple).

The importance of the opera chorus has long been determined by socioeconomic factors during the time of composition. For example, monarchs and patrons clamoring for large productions and grand spectacles required of composers great choruses. Though some choruses had little dramatic function, composers such as Gluck (again, in his work to transform opera) weaved the chorus into an important dramatic function, and that trend continues today.[1]

Chorus acting is often ignored in favor of static staging in which the chorus is expected to stand and sing (often in a big arc from stage left to stage right). Directors sometimes leave the staging of chorus scenes to the assistant stage director, further confusing the import of those scenes in the through-line of the opera. Static chorus staging leads to static scenes. Choristers and directors alike must consider that groups of people behave as a unit but always have individual motivations for doing so. Relationships in large groups are also visible when looking upon the chorus from beyond the fourth wall. A man and a woman who do not know each other but are experiencing an event together will react differently to that event and to each other than will a married couple.

Again, consider Bizet's *Carmen*. Though the chorus is made up of townspeople, cigarette factory workers, and gypsies (depending on the act), the individuals in the chorus have a relationship not only with Carmen but also with each other. They will also eventually form relationships with Don José (in act 2), and with Escamillo (in acts 2, 3, and 4) and Michaëla (in acts 1 and 3).

Good choristers, like any good performers, will not only understand the relationships that they have with the choristers around them, but also the "whys"—the motivations for the actions undertaken as a character among characters. No singer should ever consider him- or herself "just a chorus member." The most important and well-acted scenes in opera can become stagnant if the chorus is placed behind the action and simply stands and sings. "Park and bark" is as much a chorus problem as it is a principal problem. A chorus character must have a genuine reaction to what is happening on stage based on a researched backstory.

From a marketing standpoint, a young professional singer may draw the interest of a director based solely on his or her work in a chorus. The power

---

1. *The Concise Oxford Dictionary of Opera*, John Warrack and Ewan West, ed., s.v. "chorus."

of being compelling is not limited to leading roles or comprimario roles. It is always better to give too much and have a director say, "I like your energy but dial it back," than it is to give too little. However, a singer in a chorus should never "act" in order to be seen; rather, good singers will motivate their time onstage no matter how big or small they perceive their roles to be. Remember, there are no small roles, only small singers.

CHAPTER SIXTEEN

A Word About Physical Appropriateness

Many things have changed in opera over the past several decades. This book has been devoted to one particular skill that has eluded singers not born with great acting talent. However, in this rather short chapter, it is necessary to dispel some myths about opera as it is currently being cast.

There is a great elephant in the room. No one wants to discuss it. The conversation is uncomfortable and singers are defensive about it. Yet it must be dealt with. That elephant: opera is no longer an art form in which morbid obesity is acceptable. It is important at this point to note that we are not discussing a "few extra pounds." We are talking about significant weight issues. There is a tremendous difference between "overweight," "obese," and "morbidly obese," and the definitions are based on body mass index (BMI) rather than number of pounds over the average.

There is a common misconception among laypeople, but also among singers, that physical appropriateness is not a consideration when casting. There may have been, in the recent past, a time when very large singers could be cast and have exceptional careers. Most that follow opera as a matter of course know that only a few years ago, a world-famous Wagnerian soprano was fired from a major European house because she was too large to fit into the dress that was procured for her. Very soon after, said soprano had gastro-bypass surgery and lost a great deal of weight. This is *not* an extraordinary story. Not only is physical appropriateness important in casting, but so too is the cardiovascular and respiratory health of singers. When looking at a singer who is significantly overweight, not only will a director be concerned about the overall "look" of the show, but will also ask the question, "Can this singer walk up a flight of stairs and then sing the high C?"

This may not seem fair, but this is the way it is. Opera is theatre and theatre is perception. As a young singer, I was singing the role of Masetto in my first professional production of *Don Giovanni*. During a break, I asked our conductor if I should learn the role of Don Giovanni—was it something I might sing someday? The conductor replied, "You are not tall enough." I am not short by any means, but the conductor's point was that casting Don Giovanni is about a voice and a look. This seemed incredibly unfair to me, but because my height was something I couldn't really change, I had to learn to live with it.

The simple fact is that the more marketable a singer is in the current competitive climate, the better. Why would an artistic director hire a morbidly obese singer when there are ten others waiting in the hallway who sing just as well, are fit, and look the role? There is also a common misconception that men, particularly tenors and basses, can get away with almost anything because there are so few of them. To be a great artist requires sacrifice, and whether or not a singer thinks he or she has competition, there is always someone else who can sing the role and look the role. This is not to suggest that singers with beautiful voices should quit singing if they are overweight. I am also not advocating drastic weight-loss measures such as crash diets, starvation, or surgery. The only point I wish to make is this: for your own health and for your career, get to the gym.

Epilogue

M any critics and artists alike still believe that operatic acting was always meant to be *presentational*, or devoid of real emotion. Whether or not some in the operatic and arts communities wish to accept it, the art of acting has matured since the nineteenth century—theatre acting for artistic and philosophical reasons and operatic acting for practical reasons. Yet whereas Constantin Stanislavski's System for creating truthful acting radiated through the theatrical community and shaped the philosophy of acting in theatre and film from its creation to the present, there has been no operatic equivalent. Acting, as an element of opera, has seen a decline in its relevance during the twentieth century, as evidenced by, among other things, the lack of acting training offered to singers in collegiate programs. Great singer-actors have graced operatic stages, but it is likely that those singers possessed an innate acting ability or an extraordinary ability for self-study. Singers lacking this instinct have found themselves required to learn by doing, given little by way of formal acting training.

Evidence of opera's debt to drama has largely been ignored throughout recent history. This evidence includes the writings of great opera composers that would seem to contradict the idea that opera is not meant to be acted. In his preface to the opera *Alceste*, Christoph Willibald Gluck, regarded as the facilitator of operatic reforms in the eighteenth century (reforms called for by the intellectuals of the time), laid out a series of principles for the performance of opera. The first of these principles is as follows: "The music [is] to be secondary to the poetry and drama, not to weaken them by unnecessary ornaments—to be, in fact, something like the addition of colour to drawing, giving more life to the figures without changing the shapes."[1] Similarly, in his only surviving letter to soprano Aloysia Weber, dated July 30, 1778, Wolfgang Amadeus Mozart provides further insight into a composer's view of acting. In part, the letter discusses her preparation of "Ah lo previdi," a *scena* for the character Andromeda that Mozart had written for her.

---

1. Percy Scholes, ed., "Opera: Gluck," *The Oxford Companion to Music* (London: Oxford University Press, 1970), 705.

I particularly advise you to pay attention to the expression marks—to think carefully about the meaning and the force of the words—to put yourself with all seriousness into Andromeda's situation and position!—and to imagine yourself to be that very person. By doing this, with your beautiful voice—your beautiful way of singing—you will become unfailingly Excellent within a short Time![2]

Giuseppe Verdi's letters also provide the modern reader a glimpse into his priorities with regard to operatic performers. In his book *Performance Practice: A Dictionary-guide for Musicians,* Roland John Jackson wrote of these priorities: "Verdi esteemed especially power, clarity of pronunciation, and acting ability. Concerning *Don Carlo,* he wrote. 'Tell me about the quality and power of their style of singing, their enunciation, and above all their acting (letter, 11 Jan 1868).'"[3] For Verdi, his staging instructions often illuminate his opinions on the subject. Karen Henson, in an article for the *Cambridge Opera Journal,* makes the following observation: "Verdi's staging manual for *Otello* in fact urges actorly 'naturalezza' ('naturalness')."[4]

Finally, Walter Felsenstein, founder and artistic director of the Komische Oper in East Berlin, provided the most succinct argument for the equalization of the elements of opera when describing his own approach:

In giving equal weight to "music" and "theater," I was trying to remove the dividing line that exists between the terms "opera" and "theater." The working principles that came out of this were not my invention. Rather, they represented the sum total of efforts that were decades, even centuries, old and that are discussed, for example, in letters by Gluck, Verdi, and Tchaikovsky, who rebelled against the "concert in costume," the vanity of the singers, and the "routine" presentation of opera.[5]

Despite such evidence to support the claim that opera was intended to be an art form made up of equal parts, opera has long been considered, by a seeming majority, a musical art form rather than a theatrical art form. *New York Times* theatre critic Charles Isherwood provides some evidence of this

2. Robert Spaethling, ed. and trans., *Mozart's Letters, Mozart's Life: Selected Letters* (New York: Norton, 2000), 171–172.

3. Roland John Jackson, *Performance Practice: A Dictionary-Guide for Musicians* (New York: Routledge, 2005), 433.

4. Karen Henson, "Verdi, Victor Maurel and *fin-de-siècle* Operatic Performance," *Cambridge Opera Journal* 19 (2007): 65–66.

5. Walter Felsenstein, "Notes on the Komische Oper of East Berlin," *Yale/Theatre* 6 (1975): 6

opinion in a 2007 article entitled "Operatic Acting? Oxymoron No More":

> Opera was born as a radical new form incorporating music and drama, but the partnership between the elements has been an uneasy and unequal one, with musical values having taken firm precedence through much of the art form's history. For impresarios and generally for audiences too, superlative singing has always been considered to be of paramount importance.[6]

Isherwood's observation notwithstanding, it is difficult to generalize what is of "paramount importance" to an audience. It is clear, however, that market conditions are providing new competition for opera and resulting in a desire to improve all aspects of the art form in order to stay competitive. For the singer, this requires a new focus on acting in addition to singing.

Though it is not necessary to neglect the techniques and artistry of singing in order to create a truthful and meaningful interpretation of an operatic role, it is necessary to find balance. It could never be argued that the demands of singing do not require great diligence. In the recent past, a singer would be forgiven for a subpar acting performance if he or she could deliver an extraordinary musical and vocal presentation. One of the most famous examples of such a singer was Luciano Pavarotti, whose vocal artistry simply overshadowed his absolute lack of acting ability. This fact was not lost on the famous tenor, who laughed off bad acting reviews. And why not? Pavarotti made millions "parking and barking."

Given that the most famous singers of the last generation were not required to be great (or even competent) actors, it is understandable that young singers hoping to make a name for themselves spend little or no time attempting to improve their acting skills. After all, opera is an art form that looks back more than it looks forward—that prizes the past over the present and future. For the singer working toward a professional singing career, competition for roles is likely to grow. Presenting oneself only as a good singer is simply no longer enough. Why would an artistic director hire just a good singer when he or she is presented with a good singer and good actor in the same person?

In the nonlyric theatre, Constantin Stanislavski worked to create a more organic approach to acting and later found his way into the realm of the lyric stage. Though Stanislavski worked in the operatic field and even developed a company of singers, his methods, and more importantly the rehearsal

---

6. Isherwood, "Operatic Acting?"

time needed to create realistic opera acting (especially in this modern era of bottom lines), may be unrealistic. Walter Felsenstein was known to rehearse productions for up to a year and cancel performances if a singer, even in a minor role, became ill. Felsenstein felt that introducing a new singer to the production so late in the process would destroy the cohesion of the production and the comfort level of the cast, rendering the production less truthful:[7]

> The realization of our aspirations requires a careful examination of every stage work to see that the music and dramatic action are truly complementary . . . It prohibits any mere "guest appearance" of a star singer as well as any change in cast without our usual rehearsal period.[8]

Shrinking budgets are now requiring opera companies to shorten rehearsal periods in order to save money. This makes it necessary for singers to prepare their roles more thoroughly (both musically and theatrically) in order to be successful. There is in this preparation, however, a balancing act that should be carefully navigated. Singers will find that understanding the goals of their acting performances, becoming intimately familiar with the concepts of truthful acting, and preparing and rehearsing with an eye toward a goal of truthful presentation through emotional connection and commitment will improve the depths of their performances. This work, in turn, will ultimately lead to continued acclaim and employment. Acting preparation occurs simultaneously with musical preparation. Even the most successful singers should use use every rehearsal and performance as yet another opportunity in which to strive toward a perfect balance between beautiful acting and beautiful singing.

---

7. Felsenstein, "Notes," 7.
8. Ibid., 6.

Selected Bibliography

Adler, Stella. "The Stanislavski System. 1934." Stella Adler and Harold Clurman Papers. Harry Ransom Center, University of Texas at Austin. Illustration.

————. *The Technique of Acting*. New York: Bantam, 1990.

Adorno, Theodor. "Opera and the Long-Playing Record." Translated by Thomas Levin. *October* 55 (1990): 62–66.

Anthony, James R. "Opera." In *The New Grove Dictionary of Music and Musicians*, vol. 18, edited by Stanley Sadie. London: Macmillan, 2001.

Austin, Gilbert. *Chironomia; or, A Treatise on Rhetorical Delivery: Comprehending Many Precepts, Both Ancient and Modern, for the Proper Regulation of the Voice, the Countenance, and Gesture*. London: T. Cadell and W. Davies, 1806.

Bailey, Mark. *Notes on the Meisnerian Method*. Stella Adler and Harold Clurman Papers. Harry Ransom Center, University of Texas at Austin.

Balk, H. Wesley. *The Complete Singer-Actor: Training for Music Theater*. Minneapolis: University of Minnesota Press, 1985.

Bartow, Arthur, ed. *Training of the American Actor*. New York: Theatre Communications, 2006.

Benedetti, Jean. *Stanislavski and the Actor*. New York: Routledge, 1998.

Bilgrave, Dyer P. and Robert H. Deluty. "Stanislavski Acting Method and Control Theory: Commonalities across Time, Place, and Field." *Social Behavior and Society* 32 (2004): 329–340.

Bizet, Georges. *Carmen*. New York: Schirmer, 1923.

Blumenfeld, Robert. *Blumenfeld's Dictionary of Acting and Show Business.* New York: Limelight Editions: 2009.

————. *Tools and Techniques for Character Interpretation; A Handbook of Psychology for Actors, Writers, and Directors.* New York: Limelight, 2006.

————. *Using the Stanislavsky System: A Practical Guide to Character Creation & Period Styles.* Limelight Editions: New York, 2008.

Boleslavsky, Robert. *Acting: The First Six Lessons.* New York: Theatre Arts Books, 1956.

Burgess, Thomas. *The Singing and Acting Handbook: Games and Exercises for the Performer.* New York: Routledge, 2000.

Castel, Nico. *French Opera Libretti.* Vol. 1, *Werther.* Mt. Morris, NY: Leyerle, 1999.

————. *German Miscellaneous Opera Libretti.* Mt. Morris, NY: Leyerle, 2005.

Challis, Bennett. "The Technique of Operatic Acting." *The Musical Quarterly* 13 (1927): 630–645.

Clark, Mark Ross. *Singing, Acting, and Movement in Opera: A Guide to Singer-getics.* Bloomington: Indiana University Press, 2002.

Curtiss, Mina Kirstein. *Bizet and His World.* New York: Knopf, 1958.

Delaumosne, L'Abbé, Angélique Arnaud, François Delsarte, Frances A. Shaw, and Abby Langdon Alger. *Delsarte System of Oratory.* New York: Werner, 1887.

Dibbern, Mary. *Carmen: A Performance Guide.* Hillsdale: Pendragon, 2000.

Duerr, Edwin. *The Length and Depth of Acting.* New York: Holt, Rinehart and Winston, 1962.

Easty, Edward Dwight. *On Method Acting.* New York: Ballantine, 1992.

Emerson, Ralph Waldo. "Self-Reliance," *Essays, First and Second Series.* Boston: Houghton Mifflin, 1883.

Felsenstein, Walter. "Notes on the Komische Oper of East Berlin." *Yale/ Theatre* 6 (1975): 6–7.

Fisher, Burton D. *A History of Opera: Milestones and Metamorphoses.* Miami: Opera Journeys, 2005.

Freud, Sigmund, James Strachey, Anna Freud, and Carrie Lee. *Sigmund Freud; The Standard Edition of the Complete Psychological Works of Sigmund Freud.* Hogarth: London, 1955.

Fuchs, Peter Paul, ed. *The Music Theatre of Walter Felsenstein.* London: Quartet, 1991.

Gelb, Peter. "The Future of Opera." Lecture given at the Chautauqua Institution, Chautauqua, NY, August 17, 2007. MP3 downloadable from http://www.thegreatlecturelibrary.com.

Goldovsky, Boris. *Bringing Opera to Life: Operatic Acting and Stage Direction.* New York: Appleton-Century-Crofts, 1968.

Graf, Herbert. *Opera for the People.* Minneapolis: University of Minnesota Press, 1951.

Greenspan, Charlotte. "Opera." In *The Harvard Dictionary of Music,* edited by Don Michael Randel. Cambridge: Belknap, 2003.

Griffiths, Paul and Nicholas Temperly. "Opera." In *The Oxford Companion to Music,* edited by Allison Latham, 863–889. Oxford: Oxford University Press, 2002.

Grout, Donald J. *A Short History of Opera, Third Edition.* New York: Columbia University Press, 1988.

Hagen, Uta. *A Challenge for the Actor.* New York: Maxwell Macmillan International, 1991.

———. *Respect for Acting.* New York: Wiley, 1973.

Helfgot, Daniel and William O. Beeman. *The Third Line: The Opera Performer as Interpreter.* New York: Schirmer Books, 1993.

Henson, Karen. "Verdi, Victor Maurel and *fin-de-siècle* Operatic Performance." *Cambridge Opera Journal* 19 (2007): 59–84.

Hethmon, Robert H., ed. *Strasberg at the Actors Studio: Tape-Recorded Sessions.* New York: Theatre Communications Group, 1965.

Isherwood, Charles. "Operatic Acting? Oxymoron No More." *New York Times,* September 9, 2007.

Jackson, Roland John. *Performance Practice: A Dictionary-Guide for Musicians.* New York: Routledge, 2005.

Jelgerhuis, Johannes. *Theoretische lessen over de gesticulatie en mimiek.* Amsterdam: Warnars, 1827.

Kazan, Elia. *Kazan on Directing.* Vintage: New York, 2010.

Kennedy, Michael, ed., "Opera." In *The Oxford Dictionary of Music.* Oxford: Oxford University Press, 1994.

King, Richard G. "How to be an Emperor: Acting Alexander the Great in Opera Seria." *Early Music* 36 (2008): 181–201.

Kirby, E. T. "The Delsarte Method: 3 Frontiers of Actor Training." *The Drama Review: TDR* 16 (March 1972): 55–69.

Magarshack, David. *Stanislavsky, A Life.* New York: Chanticleer, 1951.

Maslow, Abraham. "A Theory of Human Motivation." In *Twentieth century Psychology: Recent Developments in Psychology,* edited by Philip Harriman, 22–48. New York: Philosophical Library, 1946.

Meisner, Sanford and Martin Barter. *Sanford Meisner Master Class.* Directed by Sydney Pollack. 460 min. Los Angeles: Open Road Films, 2006. DVD.

Merlin, Bella. *The Complete Stanislavski Toolkit*. Hollywood: Drama Publishers, 2007.

Metten, Charles. "Artist and Lawgiver of the Russian Stage." *Educational Theatre Journal* 14 (March 1962): 44–49.

Meyer-Dinkgräfe, Daniel. *Approaches to Acting; Past and Present*. New York: Continuum, 2005.

Moore. Sonia. *The Stanislavski System*. New York: Penguin, 1977.

Moss, Larry. *The Intent to Live: Achieving Your True Potential as an Actor*. New York: Bantam Dell, 2006.

Mozart, Wolfgang Amadeus. *Die Zauberflöte*. Bonn: Simrock, 1793.

Nagy, Gregor. *The Best of the Achaeans*. Baltimore: Johns Hopkins University Press, 1979.

National Association of Schools of Music. *Handbook 2009–2010*. Reston: National Association of Schools of Music, 2008.

Ostwald, David F. *Acting for Singers: Creating Believable Singing Characters*. Oxford: Oxford University Press, 2005.

Palisca, Claude V. "Bardi, Giovanni de', Count of Vernio." In *Grove Music Online*. Accessed May 7, 2010. http://www.oxfordmusiconline.com/ subscriber/article/grove/music/02033.

Palisca, Claude V. "Camerata." In *Grove Music Online*. Accessed May 17, 2010. http://www.oxfordmusiconline.com:80/subscriber/article/grove/ music/0462.

Park, Lawrence. *Since Stanislavski and Vakhtangov: The Method as a System for* Today's *Actor*. Hollywood: Acting World Books, 1985.

Pitches, Jonathan. *Science and the Stanislavsky Tradition of Acting*. New York: Routledge, 2006.

Redgrave, Michael. *The Actor's Ways and Means*. London: W. Heinemann, 1953.

Rossini, Gioachino. *Il barbiere di Siviglia*. New York: Schirmer, 1900.

Ruyter, Nancy Lee Chalfa. *The Cultivation of Body and Mind in Nineteenth-Century American Delsartism*. Westport, CT: Greenwood, 1999.

Sadie, Stanley. *History of Opera*. New York: W. W. Norton, 1990.

Savage, Roger. "Staging an Opera: Letters from the Caesarian Poet." *Early Music* 26 (1998): 583–595.

Schechner, Richard. "Magnitudes of performance." In *By Means of Performance: Intercultural Studies of Theatre and Ritual*, edited by Richard Schechner and Willa Appel, 19–49. New York: Cambridge University Press, 1997.

Scheeder, Louis. "Strasberg's Method and the Ascendancy of American Acting." In *Training of the American Actor*, edited by Arthur Bartow, 3–13. New York: Theatre Communications, 2006.

Scheier, Michael, and Charles Carver. "A Model of Behavioral Self-Regulation: Translating Intention into Action." In *Advances in Experimental Social Psychology*, vol. 21, edited by Leonard Berkowitz. San Diego: Academic Press, 1988.

Scholes, Percy, ed. "Opera: Gluck." *The Oxford Companion to Music*, 10th Edition. London: Oxford University Press, 1970.

Shakespeare, William. *The Works of William Shakespeare; Measure for Measure*. Edited by H. C. Hart. London: Metheun, 1905.

Shea, George E. *Acting in Opera*. London: Schirmer, 1915.

Silverberg, Larry. *The Sanford Meisner Approach: An Actor's Workbook*. New Hampshire: Smith and Kraus, 1994.

Soloviova, Vera, Stella Adler, Sanford Meisner, and Paul Gray. "The Reality of Doing." *The Tulane Drama Review* 9, No. 1 (Autumn, 1964): 136–155.

Spaethling, Robert, ed. and trans. *Mozart's Letters, Mozart's Life: Selected Letters.* New York: Norton, 2000.

Stanislavski, Constantin. *An Actor Prepares.* Translated and edited by Elizabeth Reynolds Hapgood. New York: Theatre Arts, 1961.

———. *Creating a Role.* Translated by Elizabeth Reynolds Hapgood. New York: Theatre Arts, 1989.

———. *My Life in Art.* New York: Routledge, 1987.

———. *Stanislavski's Legacy.* Translated and edited by Elizabeth Reynolds Hapgood. London: Max Reinhardt, 1958.

Stanislavski, Constantin, and Pavel Rumyantsev. *Stanislavski on Opera.* Translated and edited by Elizabeth Reynolds Hapgood. New York: Theatre Arts Books, 1975.

Stanislavsky, Constantin. *My Life in Art.* Translated by J. J. Robbins. Boston: Little, Brown, and Company, 1924.

Stanislavsky, Konstantin. *My Life in Art.* Translated by J. J. Robbins. New York: Theatre Arts Books, 1948.

Stebbins, Genevieve. *Delsarte System of Expression.* New York: Werner, 1902.

The Lee Strasberg Theatre and Film Institute website. "Our Background." Accessed April 10, 2010. http://strasberg.com/lstfi/index. php?option=com_content&view=article&id=201&ltemid=103.

Strohm, Reinhard. *Dramma per musica: Italian Opera Seria of the Eighteenth Century.* New Haven: Yale University Press, 1997.

Titchener, E. B. "Affective Memory." *The Philosophical Review* 4, No. 1 (Jan. 1895): 65–76.

Twining, Thomas. *Aristotle's Treatise on Poetry.* London: McDowall, 1815.

Wagner, Richard. *Opera and Drama.* Translated by William Ashton Ellis. Lincoln: University of Nebraska, 1995.

Warrack, John, and Ewan West. *The Concise Oxford Dictionary of Opera,* s.v. "chorus." Oxford: Oxford University Press, 1996.

Weiss, Piero. *Opera: A History in Documents.* New York: Oxford University Press, 2002.

Index